T0360620

"This book offers a comprehensive review of the leadership and management literature. In addition, it tells the story of leaders, including the author, who have given their lives to caring for and protecting the natural resources that we all hold in common. We owe them all a debt of gratitude."

Peter Block, *Organization Development Consultant, Author, The Empowered Manager*

"Fred Cubbage is as frank, as he is knowledgeable. Bucking the closed door, top only, leadership style, he instead trusts the entire team with an open door and open plan to align vision and achieve success. Cubbage brings decades of natural resource experience with him as he shares within Natural Resource Leadership and Management for Practitioners, a thoughtful compendium on best practices in natural resource leadership."

Mary Ellen Aronow, *Director, Forest Economics, Hancock Natural Resource Group*

"Because we like nature we are taking up natural resource leadership. Fred Cubbage draws this conclusion out of his life experience that is full of active engagement in forestry. Being a brilliant researcher Fred shows well applicable, science-based tactics for leaders and illustrates those by lively examples. A great book to become better prepared for jumping into leadership challenges wherever you are in your career!"

Max Krott, *Professor for Forest and Nature Conservation Policy, Georg-August University of Göttingen, Germany*

"In this book, Dr. Cubbage has provides a valuable collection of principles and perspectives on leadership in natural resources that have not existed before. First, it is the confluence of two scholarly rivers, one being key principles from iconic management gurus and the other being key philosophies of iconic conservation leaders. Second, it details his personal applications of these principles and philosophies through his life as an honored practitioner, manager and leader in natural resources and in several contexts. In this way, his book is also a rare glimpse into the real-world trials and travails of an everyday leader who chose to step into the arena in the finest tradition of Teddy Roosevelt and Gifford Pinchot."

Tom Davidson, *Forester, MBA, MS Organizational Development,*
Leadership Nature

"In times like today, times of great change, natural resource practitioners must cultivate — intentionally grow — their personal abilities to lead people and manage resources well. Highly effective skills to lead and manage well are needed now more than ever in natural resource-related professions. I highly recommend this book for that personal cultivation and growth, but I recommend the book specifically for facilitated, small group or class discussions. The insights provided are best internalized by facilitated discussions followed by personal reflection, which is high octane fuel for personal growth in this essential field."

Steve Bullard, *former forestry professor, department chair, and dean,*
and recently retired as provost, Stephen F. Austin State University

Fred Cubbage provides a thoughtful examination of organizational management as well as his own examples of leadership applications in forestry and natural resources. Fred has succinctly highlighted honest cases of challenges that other conscientious natural resource professionals are likely to encounter during their career, as well as pitfalls and rewards associated with their leadership. An excellent read for any professional looking to improve their leadership skills while fulfilling their broader mission in the environmental field.

Christa Rogers, *Natural Resource Manager, Mecklenburg County*
Parks System

"Armed with about four decades of professional involvement, Dr. Cubbage communicates about many natural resource management phenomena. Based on case studies, he perceptively analyzes practitioners' pragmatic management and leadership roles. For multidimensional natural resources' attributes, the distinguished economist developed a simplified leadership and management model and examined key scenarios: Identify missions, develop objectives and strategies, develop infrastructure, employ and lead personnel, measure performance, and evaluate success."

Chris Zinkhan, *Chairman, The Forestland Group*

"The book, Natural Resource Policy, written by Fred Cubbage and others has become the standard for teaching policy to undergraduate resource management students for many years. This new book takes the lessons gained from the first book and provides students with the tools to engage in the development and implementation of resource policy. The main examples in the book are gleaned from the author's personal experience and provide a fascinating array of problems that resource managers and administrators are likely to face in their careers. A great introduction to the ideas of leadership that many will benefit from."

David H. Newman, *Interim Provost and Vice President of Academic Affairs, SUNY College of Environmental Science and Forestry (ESF)*

"Professor Cubbage delivers a masterpiece on natural resources leadership. The book fills a critical void in the literature, adding academic gravitas to a topic usually left to conservation activists, and folding natural resources into a subject usually left to the business school crowd. Topics like "Shady Approaches" and "Wicked Problems" offer the reader a sobering look at common leadership pitfalls, and highlights the need for the leadership models, principles, and tools that Cubbage shares.

The work is robust and thoughtful, drawing on Professor Cubbage's deep understanding of natural resources policy and informed by his many years of professional and academic leadership. The book is surprisingly accessible while delivering depth of understanding (and great stories) that will delight leadership beginners and experts alike.

Students of policy, management, and leadership will find Cubbage engaging while imparting decades of practical wisdom with relative ease and without pretention. The combination of powerful stories to inform and reinforce key concepts and accessible writing will make this a standard guide for a new generation of leaders trying to make sense of a complex and complicated system. Aspiring leaders would be wise to add Cubbage to their reading list."

Damian C. Adams, *Ph.D., J.D., Professor, Natural Resource Policy & Economics, Associate Dean for Research, University of Florida*

Natural Resource Leadership and Management

This book examines leadership and management in natural resources, drawing on literature, principles, and the author's own experiences as a leader and activist.

Developing a general framework summarizing the leadership and management cycle in natural resources for practitioners, the book provides a synthesis of leadership theory and practice stemming from the personal and spiritual values of work, and the key principle of aligning organizational resources and actions with stated intentions. It discusses the somewhat unique context of natural resources, comprised of private and public goods and services and complex societal values. Key strategies that enable natural resource professionals to be leaders at all stages and positions in their career, including vision and sustainability, proficient human resources management, fairness and merit, and transparency and openness are analyzed. Case studies of famous natural resource leaders and activists, including Ding Darling, David Attenborough, Wangari Maathai, Marina de Silva, Greta Thunberg, Bob Brown, and Christina Koch, are included. The book examines their values, training, and principles and how they influenced national or global natural resource management. Drawing on the author's own experiences as a leader and activist, including his role as Department Head at North Carolina State University, as an elected officer in the Society of American Foresters, and as an activist opposing the sale of the Hofmann Forest, the book provides practical examples and guidelines that professionals can consider and use in their careers.

This book will be of great interest to natural resource managers and professionals as well as students studying environmental management and natural resource governance and to practitioners who are looking to develop broader leadership and management skills.

Frederick Cubbage is Professor in the Department of Forestry and Environmental Resources at North Carolina State University, USA. He has been a line manager or elected leader with several organizations for two decades and is an author or coauthor of more than 500 scientific articles and several books.

Routledge Focus on Environment and Sustainability

For more information about this series, please visit: www.routledge.com/ Routledge-Focus-on-Environment-and-Sustainability/book-series/RFES

Natural Resource Leadership and Management
A Practical Guide for Professionals

Frederick Cubbage

Routledge
Taylor & Francis Group

LONDON AND NEW YORK

First published 2022
by Routledge
2 Park Square, Milton Park, Abingdon, Oxon OX14 4RN

and by Routledge
605 Third Avenue, New York, NY 10158

Routledge is an imprint of the Taylor & Francis Group, an informa business

British Library Cataloguing-in-Publication Data
A catalogue record for this book is available from the British Library

Library of Congress Cataloging-in-Publication Data
Names: Cubbage, Frederick W. author.
Title: Natural resource leadership and management : a practical guide for professionals / Frederick Cubbage.
Description: Abingdon, Oxon ; New York, NY : Routledge, 2022. | Series: Routledge focus on environment and sustainability | Includes bibliographical references and index.
Identifiers: LCCN 2021037253 (print) | LCCN 2021037254 (ebook) | ISBN 9780367692971 (hbk) | ISBN 9780367693008 (pbk) | ISBN 9781003141297 (ebk)
Subjects: LCSH: Natural resources—Management. | Leadership. | Management—Environmental aspects.
Classification: LCC HC85 .C83 2022 (print) | LCC HC85 (ebook) | DDC 333.7068—dc23
LC record available at https://lccn.loc.gov/2021037253
LC ebook record available at https://lccn.loc.gov/2021037254

ISBN: 978-0-367-69297-1 (hbk)
ISBN: 978-0-367-69300-8 (pbk)
ISBN: 978-1-003-14129-7 (ebk)

DOI: 10.4324/9781003141297

To Rita, of Course

Contents

Illustrations

Figures

Tables

Preface

This book is about natural resource leadership and management for practitioners, by a practitioner. While there are a moderate number of books and articles about natural resource leadership, they are more often written from a theoretical viewpoint. In contrast, I focus on the middle ground of presenting some theory and key principles based on general management literature, coupled with articles and books about natural resources leadership, complemented by my personal and professional experience of about four decades.

Summarizing and encapsulating natural resource management and leadership in one brief book is, of course, a bit heroic, but hopefully I can provide some salient insights on an important subject for professionals, for whom there is little sanguine opinion or relevant research. There are thousands of management and leadership books, and in fact the genre purportedly is second only to religion in total book sales. So it could be difficult to pick a primary theme, summarize and present it well, and defend it from the host of other views and experts. Nonetheless, this brief book surely provides a unique overview and perspective that should provoke interest and reflection and add to the natural resource leadership literature.

As observed in a book on environmental leadership by Gordon and Berry (2006), my view is that of a practitioner, who has managed and led organizations and advocacy efforts, in addition to serving for decades as a scholar of policy and social science research and observer of leaders. My management and leadership experiences resemble those stated by Deans John Gordon and Joyce Berry who write that in their "ordinary" academic leadership roles, they "have hired and fired; delighted and infuriated employees, clients, and the general public; seen our leadership praised and criticized."

Drawing from those two former distinguished Deans, my management experiences as a Department Head have been even more ordinary compared to globally famous environmental leaders. But we all have advanced beyond the norm for our professions. There are probably only 50 or less natural resource Deans at any given time, and a couple of hundred natural resource Department Heads. I also was one of a select group who has advanced to the highest level of President in our professional Society of American Foresters (SAF) and one of only a few persons I know who has actively co-led an environmental campaign to reverse a decision of their employer. So I have advanced moderately in my career but am far from famous.

My leadership and management experiences have been extensive and challenging—and not far from the trenches—providing experiences and insights typical of many natural resource professionals. I worked with and led small organizational units or research project teams of up to 10 persons for three decades, both as a USDA Forest Service Project Leader for 3 years and as a professor for 40 years. I was a coinvestigator on more than 100 external grants, averaging about a half million dollars per year, and a coauthor of more than 500 publications and several books on natural resource policy and forest economics. I was the founder and codirector for 25 years of the Southern Forest Resource Assessment Consortium (SOFAC), a forest economics and market modeling research co-op that grew to 25 forest industry, state, and consulting members.

I served as Head of the North Carolina State University (NCSU) Department of Forestry and Environmental Resources for 10 years. While Head, I led and managed more than 50 talented—but resolutely independent—faculty members as direct reports, and about 50 other full-time employees; more than 100 temporary employees, student workers, graduate research assistants; and hundreds of students. In addition, I had ultimate management responsibility for 5,000 acres of forest land; about a dozen vintage trucks, vans, and two buses; a resident summer camp with approximately 20 cabins, classrooms, and a dining hall, attended by 60 or more teenage men and a few women; and managed a $5 million to $10 million annual budget. To quote one of my predecessors, the job as Head of the Department of Forestry was "just one damn thing after another." One of my successors said they wished it were just *one* thing at a time.

My middle management colleagues in industry and government have expressed similar sentiments about their management challenges, as well as, of course, their enjoyment of their respective professions, and the leadership opportunities we were provided. I learned Spanish passably when I was about 50 and served as Fulbright Scholar for 6 months in Argentina and Uruguay; consulted for private sector firms and business associations and the World Bank for about 20 years in the United States, Latin America, and Asia; and developed long-term and long-distance research projects with about 20 scientists in a dozen or so countries.

In my line positions with the Forest Service and at NC State, I participated in intensive professional management training and leadership courses and attended management seminars, diversity training, and supervisor training modules. I developed skills through reading management and leadership books such as Hersey and Blanchard (1982), Block (1987, 2017), Covey (1990), Phillips (1992), Collins (2001), and Laughlin and Andringa (2007). I have taken various short management courses (Lilly Teaching Fellows, USDA Forest Service Policy Management, Carnegie Mellon College Management, a Covey course, various management supervisor trainings, and diversity courses); read biographies and autobiographies about conservation heroes such as Theodore Roosevelt (1913), Gifford Pinchot (1947), Aldo Leopold (1949), and Ding Darling (Lendt 1978); and had perpetual discussions with and observations of other managers. I also have subscribed to *Fortune* and *The Economist* for several decades and read almost every management article in those publications.

In addition to line management and leadership employment experience, I served as a technical committee chairperson, member, or stakeholder representative on three nongovernment forest certification organizations for a decade and helped set or review their forest certification standards. As a career-long professional member and volunteer in our professional SAF, I served at least 15 years in volunteer technical/staff roles with increasing responsibility as a newsletter editor, a technical working group chair, a science board member, a journal associate editor, and educational accreditation committee member.

I served another dozen years with SAF as an elected officer in governance/line positions that included setting policies and helping or leading in setting annual budgets ranging from a few thousand dollars to several million dollars. I was a chapter and a state chairperson for SAF, chairing challenging and profitable state and national conventions and programs; was a national governing council representative; and eventually was elected President. I also served as a voluntary coleader of an environmental campaign, in which I had a role as an internal and external activist opposing a decision made by my employer to sell our 79,000-acre Hofmann Forest, a role perhaps similar to that of a whistleblower.

All of these employment and volunteer leadership roles provided plenty of leadership opportunities, problems, and terror, with personnel, financial challenges, and contention—as well as considerable satisfaction and lifelong friends—and never seemed ordinary or dull. Furthermore, the leadership experience supplemented my official management training, both in those jobs and in the profession. These experiences and the insights I offer here might well be at levels not so different than many other natural resource professionals who I have met in my career and therefore provide a valuable summary of management and leadership principles and practice.

The purpose of a leadership and management book for natural resources is captured well by Block (2017) in his inspiring book *The Empowered Manager* (p. xxiii):

> At its best a book represents the beginning of a journey for the reader, but it represents the coming together, even closure, of a journey for the author. As in teaching, you write about those things you care about but don't quite understand, hoping that the act and stress of putting things on paper for public view will give you the clarity you yearn for.

I will focus on leadership principles and experiences from the early phases in one's career to middle levels of natural resource organizations, not on providing encyclopedic digests of theories and approaches, which are covered well in other literature, much of which is referenced here. This primer examines how leadership and management can occur and succeed in natural resources organizations, which can provide a useful introduction to the subject for professionals, introduce interested managers and leaders to some of the key principles, and suggest more comprehensive references. This book also provides three specific case studies in natural resources and occasional pragmatic comments based on my experience, which are more tangible than general theories from persons farther afield.

It is tempting to fill this book with innumerable ideas and lists about leadership in order to appear more academic, but there is cap on the number of words allowed in this brief primer, and too many references alone would make me exceed it. So I focus on key subjects and literature relevant to ordinary leaders in natural resources such as myself. To some extent, this book is a simplification of various complex and encyclopedic tomes common in academia; it is instead more similar to popular management books.

Colin Powell is often quoted as stating that a great leader is a master of simplification, who can cut through argument, debate, and doubt to offer a solution everybody can understand (Harari 2005). One might draw that analogy for this book, which is hopefully well reasoned and illustrated thoroughly with examples, but not overwhelming. I will let you all as readers and users determine if I have achieved that goal, as well as providing substantive, practical, and useful insights about leadership and management in natural resources.

References

Block P. 1987. *The Empowered Manager: Positive Political Skills at Work.* San Francisco (CA): Jossey-Bass Publishers. 214 p.

Block P. 2017. *The Empowered Manager, Second Edition: Positive Political Skills at Work.* Hoboken (NJ): Wiley. 213 p.

Collins J. 2001. *Good to Great.* New York: Harper Business. 320 p.

Covey SR. 1990. *Principle-Centered Leadership.* New York: Free Press. 335 p.

Gordon JC, Berry JK. 2006. *Environmental Leadership Equals Essential Leadership: Redefining Who Leads and How.* New Haven (CT): Yale University Press. 164 p.

Harari O. 2005. *The Powell Principles.* New York: McGraw-Hill. 116 p.

Hersey P, Blanchard KH. 1982. *Management of Organizational Behavior: Utilizing Human Resources.* Englewood Cliffs (NJ): Prentice Hall. 343 p.

Laughlin FL, Andringa RC. 2007. *Good Governance for Nonprofits.* New York: American Management Association. 210 p.

Lendt DL. 1978. Ding: The life of Jay Norwood Darling [retrospective dissertation 6464]. [Ames (IA)]: Iowa State University. Available at: https://lib.dr.iastate.edu/rtd/6464. Accessed 21 January 2021.

Leopold A. 1949. *Sand County Almanac, Arizona and New Mexico: Thinking Like a Mountain.* Oxford, England: Oxford University Press. 240 p.

Phillips DT. 1992. *Lincoln on Leadership.* New York: Grand Central Publishing. 193 p.

Pinchot G. 1947. *Breaking New Ground* [Posthumous Autobiography]. New York: Harcourt, Brace. 522 p.

Roosevelt T. 1913. *An Autobiography.* New York: Palgrave Macmillan. 615 p.

1 The Leadership and Management Cycle in Natural Resources

Introduction

We all have many opportunities to engage in leadership and management. Leadership consists of aligning an organization's resources and actions with its stated intentions. Articulating a clearly stated vision and doing what you say can move organizations forward and resolve issues. Conversely, vague or inconsistent missions, statements, and rewards systems can lead to disillusionment, reduced loyalty, and poor performance.

Good leaders do many things when successful. They identify, affirm, and implement an organizational vision and develop a strategy and tactics to achieve that vision. They listen and learn from staff and customers; discern changes that can improve the organization or community they work with; and lead new efforts to change the status quo and make improvements. Leaders try to work within existing polices, rules, and regulations to achieve success and identify and make new rules and policies to help achieve their vision. Leaders try to build collegial, effective, and enduring organizational teams and reform rules and practices to institutionalize improvements.

Leadership and management are among the most crucial components for organizational success and personal satisfaction in all disciplines. Despite its importance, there is only a modest amount of literature on leadership in natural resources, either based on research or experience. Leadership and management in natural resources are, of course, crucial as population increases; natural resources become scarcer; adverse environmental impacts continue; complex problems proliferate; and government and private budgets and personnel dwindle.

This book has chapters on elements of management, leadership principles, and case studies of natural resource leaders. This synthesis of leadership theory and practice in natural resources can identify some characteristics that define good management; assess how leaders employ leadership and management tools in order to achieve and implement desirable professional

DOI: 10.4324/9781003141297-1

missions and objectives; and illustrate how these principles, strategies, and tactics can be used by natural resource professionals. As an aside, we face a small semantic issue when we talk about natural resource management, which usually infers what plans and practices we employ to manage and protect land and natural resources. Instead, this book focuses on personnel and organizational management, not land management per se, although the objective of our professions is indeed to manage land and its resources as well for social benefits.

Unlike most physical (e.g., gravity), biological sciences (e.g., evolution), or even economics as a social science (e.g., neoclassical economics), there is no unified golden theory of leadership in natural resources or any other discipline. I do present some principles about and practices of good leadership here; discuss a synthesis of management and leadership research, classic and current leadership books, and popular literature; and draw on a few famous conservation leaders and my experience to develop a holistic view of leadership and management in natural resources. This book will cover professionalism, work, careers, and the uniqueness of the natural resource context for leaders and managers. I will present a general model of management and leadership in this chapter that has six key elements, which I discuss in part in the following chapters.

Leadership versus Management

Drawing from Peter Block (1987, 2017) in *The Empowered Manager*, leadership can be defined as aligning an organization's resources and actions with their stated intentions, which will be one foundation in this book. Modern natural resource management provides many unique challenges for leaders, including the intertwined nature of both market goods and ecosystem services; the challenge of managing across private and public institutions; and the increased focus on more inclusion of diverse stakeholders, interest groups, and people in making such management decisions. Natural resource organizations must also attract and reward talent in competition with other better-paying sectors; garner profits and demonstrate environmental, social, and governance (ESG) components for private companies; and usually deal with at best stable to decreasing budgets for public agencies.

There is some debate about the difference between leadership and management, and some agreement that they are two components of any successful organization or individual. Leadership may be identified with perceiving and pursuing the best courses of actions for an organization and uniting and motivating people. Management involves planning and budgeting, organizing and assigning work and solving problems, and encouraging and controlling processes (Štreimikienė et al. 2020). A commonly cited adage by

Peter Drucker (2001) states that "leaders do the right thing and managers do the thing right." This unnecessarily disparages managers and too narrowly circumscribes leaders. Management is about coping with complexity in increasingly large organizations in order to ensure the quality and profitability of products or services. Leadership, by contrast, is about coping with change—technological, competition, changing demographics, changing values, and many more factors (Kotter 1990).

Successful individuals and organizations must always do both components of management and leadership well in order to prosper, grow, improve, and endure. Managers must understand an organization's mission, objectives, culture, people, resources, and limitations in order to perform their tasks effectively. Leaders need to think creatively, learn from managers and employees, communicate effectively, and model dedication and commitment to the vision of an organization. Good managers and good leaders occur at all levels of an organization, and effective contributors use their mix of talents, skills, training, and teamwork to be workers, managers, and leaders at various times in their occupations and careers.

Leadership can, with difficulty, help an organization and an individual achieve their mutual mission and goals and get the right things done well. Leaders set the discussion and action agenda for accomplishing the right things, with the right people, and through the right approaches. They will improve the management and practices for natural resource use and protection. By performing work well in their organization, leaders also will improve their lives, spirits, and self-actualization. They can help organizations fulfill their stated missions, by aligning what they say and what they do, thus helping achieve their stated missions and intentions.

A Model of Leadership and Management

The plethora of leadership theories, books, texts, research, articles, opinions, blogs, vlogs, tweets, and more makes a unified theory of leadership and management unlikely. However, to make any progress on understanding management and leadership in natural resources, surely some guiding theory is necessary. Based on my scholarship and experience with the subject, Figure 1.1 summarizes a reasonable synthesis of six elements that private and public managers and leaders must consider and perform, either explicitly or implicitly, for their natural resource organizations.

Per my conceptual model, managers and leaders must (1) assess their organizational context and mission; (2) develop visions, objectives, and approaches to achieve the mission; (3) develop the organizational capacity for delivering products or services; (4) employ people and contractors to perform the work; (5) monitor and reward performance; and (6) evaluate

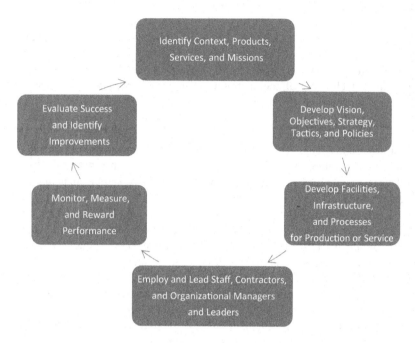

Figure 1.1 Overview of a leadership and management cycle in natural resources

success and improve the organizational processes and outputs. I use this schema to discuss leadership in natural resources in this book and focus on specifics that seem most important and useful based on the principles, scientific and popular literature, and cases. I draw on several decades of my professional experience, training, and observation as well.

Each of these broad management and leadership categories in Figure 1.1 is needed for successful management, and leaders help identify, plan, and execute actions that implement them well. In reality, all firms and organizations will in some fashion have some implicit or specific purpose for their actions and do something well enough to exist—or so badly that they fail. But management is the key to doing known tasks well, and leadership is the key to identifying what things to do well; how to motivate managers, leaders, and staff; what processes to use; who will perform the jobs; and how to work with managers and employees in order to enable the organization to achieve its mission and objectives.

While the figure is circular, each of these steps in the management and leadership cycle often is not sequential in practice, except for maybe start-up firms or new agencies. In practice all of these components of an organization are active simultaneously, although the focus of leaders will vary depending on the needs and timing of the production or service processes underway. As the diagram suggests, there are a huge number of tasks in leading and managing an organization or part of an organization. Leaders and managers cannot focus on all of these at once, so must find good employees and staff in all components of the production or service functions in order to achieve success. Let me expand briefly on each component of the management and leadership cycle here as an overview and how they relate specifically to natural resources.

Resource and Organizational Context

First, managers and leaders must identify or recognize the private or public sector context that they are in—the purpose of the organization and the types of goods and services that they produce, and its commitments to human and social needs—which form the mission of their organization. Leaders must identify the natural, human, and financial resources and constraints of their organization; the social and environmental situation they experience; the competition that they have in their markets; the problems with producing goods or services in their sector or in their organization; and the approaches needed to improve their status quo. Every business or service situation will be different in some respects, but broad sectors of business and public organizations have similar characteristics. This context then provides the structure that organizations rely on to develop their missions.

Both management and leadership can occur at every level of an organization, whether it be a private firm, a government organization, or a nonprofit enterprise. Leadership consists of seeing and understanding what should be done in a job to achieve the organization's objectives, not simply implementing routine tasks. Morgan et al. (2019) note the importance of context in transferring leadership principles and practices. Furthermore, they note that public leadership consists of "making a difference from where we sit," inferring that all professionals have opportunities for being leaders at their position in an organization and in their natural and social environments. To do this, one also must examine and understand those business, social, cultural, organizational, and natural environments.

Similarly, Bendell et al. (2018) state that we should "[r]ecognize that leader is a label and people can take acts of leadership without it meaning that they are permanent leaders." Leaders are not a unique, chosen, or emergent few, but rather many persons can be leaders, depending on the situation and the timing. One does not need to be a leader continuously, but rather for a period of time. Leadership also brings political, moral, and sustainability issues, not just managerial perspectives. Bendell et al. (2018) conclude that sustainable leadership requires ethical behavior to help people resolve shared dilemmas.

Leaders must recognize how their situation is similar to or different than others in their sector and what goals they should pursue for their particular organization. Although every business and service sector is indeed different, natural resource organizations may justly claim to be unique in their context and professions, since they deal with such a complex set of intertwined private markets and public goods and complex social networks and expectations. Natural resource professionals must discern the characteristics of their context and situation; how it is similar to or different from other resource situations or other sectors; how they can use common management tools and techniques to address problems; and when they must innovate and become leaders in order to improve situations and controversies, if not to permanently resolve them.

Vision, Objectives, Strategy, and Policies

Second, leaders and managers must innovate and develop a vision, objectives, strategies, tactics, policies, or other approaches to achieve their organization's missions. There is some continuum among these hierarchy of organizational components. Mission statements describe the purpose of an organization and what it does and the environment it operates in. In general, a vision articulates what the organization aspires to be, and objectives identify specific measurable actions required or outputs it wants to achieve (Block 2017).

Broad strategies of how to achieve a vision help focus on an organization's efforts, and tactics relate to specific actions that will be performed. At a more practical level, policies, rules, and regulations state what an organization will do in achieving and implementing their vision and objectives, providing an overlay of processes and rules for effective and equitable practices in an organization. Organizations also may have semi-formal or informal standard operating procedures, which do not rise to the level of any written rule, but still are well-understood customary approaches and practices that can be followed by local units or lower levels in an organization.

Organizational visions do not need to be innovative or new all the time. In fact, frequently creating new visions can be counterproductive. People and organizations can be whipsawed by visioning exercises and transitions every time a new leader arrives. Useful and wise organizational visions, however, will endure many leaders and managers and perhaps last for decades. Every leader should review current visions, help employees and stakeholders reaffirm, refine, or replace them based on the current context and situations, and periodically develop new goals, objectives, strategies, and tactics for their implementation.

While broad visions may be enduring, entrepreneurs and leaders must discern what great innovations that either new or existing organizations can achieve, develop methods and processes to achieve these goals, and make sure that all employees and contractors understand the program. New visions and missions surely must occur as the organizational context changes, due to new business environments and markets, new politics, new social situations, changing public demands, and more. Leaders should have a wider view of the world, and be among the first persons to perceive these needed changes, and indeed lead the organization to consider changes in their environment that should prompt changes in their missions and visions. Leaders also need to have the courage to bring these opportunities or problems to the table to foster open discussion and change.

Leaders also should be among the first to recognize when organizations stray from their traditional missions and visions or when external conditions and factors require changes. Leaders must force renewal of even forgotten purposes for their organization or for their level in an organization or adaptation to new worlds. Often managers or employees are afraid to speak out in the face of problems, and leaders must be willing to risk rejection, opposition, silence, or scorn when they bring issues out in the open but may gain respect for doing so and fostering positive change. Leaders are assisted in setting goals and objectives by their ability to build and work with managers and staff to articulate that vision and organize resources to produce such goods or services.

Facilities, Infrastructure, and Processes

Third, leaders and managers must develop the facilities, infrastructure, and processes to achieve their mission, vision, and objectives. For commodity products, organizations obviously need manufacturing plants, agricultural land, forests, mining facilities, or other tangible land or industrial infrastructure and processes. For services such as finance, leisure, recreation, or medicine, organizations may still need infrastructure, but the outputs are either wealth, enjoyment, or health. These usually require human "built" or engineered infrastructure but also often involve natural environmental "green" infrastructure.

Natural resource leaders and managers must develop or improve the built and natural infrastructure that they have; figure out how to produce an appropriate quality commodity or service well, efficiently, profitably, and responsibly; and manage and protect a natural resource sustainably. The

processes also may be sets of physical production activities or business procedures and work flows to perform service activities.

Human Resources

Fourth, organizations must employ and lead staff, contractors, consultants,
and other human resource workers and professionals to do the work and
run the organization. Aligning statements and resources must focus on the
human resources, talent, and culture to succeed. Good human resources
personnel are scarce, and successful management of people and issues is
difficult. Managers and leaders supervise full- and part-time employees
and temporary employees hired by their firm; arrange for contractors and
service providers; and interact with other private sector and government
agency officials who may affect or regulate the business practices, social
practices, or environmental compliance.

Contractors are used increasingly often in public and private organizations for efficiency and regulatory reasons. It often may be easier to give
a specific task or service to contractors who specialize in a professional,
technical, or blue-collar field. Contractors usually have specific deliverables
or tasks to perform, which makes measuring success easier. Contractors
also may help firms to avoid permanently employing excessive staffs, which
may not be fully employed during swings of activity in their business cycle.
In addition, contractors often can help companies or public agencies avoid
significant government rules and regulations or at least shift the compliance
to other firms. Smaller firms may have fewer applicable government rules
than large firms and might have more flexibility for hiring temporary workers and more ability to be independent and innovative than large organizations with more structure and rules.

In any organization and for any manager, human resources may be the
most difficult part of the job. Most leaders and managers are attracted to
their discipline by the nature of the product or the service and its intellectual
or practical work enjoyment. Most natural resource or perhaps other sector managers and employees are not attracted because of human resource
management, except indeed the HR personnel who seek such positions. So
attracting and retaining staff in fulfilling jobs with constraints of reasonable
pay, benefits, work expectations, and promotions is difficult. Managers and
HR personnel who achieve this well are far more likely to have successful
organizations.

Theories of how to manage people abound, and success is often ephemeral and difficult to measure regardless. Determining how to manage people
in natural resources is certainly no easier than in other private or public
sectors, and the complex tasks with modest pay handicap success. This may

be offset sometimes by the attraction and beauty of working outdoors in a natural environment, but sustainable livelihoods and professional esteem are important for all careers and for employee satisfaction. And even working outdoors has limitations such as heat, cold, rain, rugged, wet or inaccessible terrain, serious ticks, and infectious disease pathogens, all of which become more challenging as persons get older. Like all professions, natural resources disciplines have increased their efforts to increase their ethnic and gender diversity and inclusion, which is required to attract and retain the best talent.

Monitoring and Evaluation

Fifth, related to human resources, organizations also must monitor, measure, and reward success for delivering products and services. This is meant to measure both the outputs of the organization and the success of the manager at achieving the goals and objectives relevant at their level of the organization. Successful monitoring does require objectives that are specific enough to be measured, even if they are somewhat subjective. Targets such as production quantities, visitor days, costs, and employee satisfaction, absence, or turnover all are metrics that can be employed to measure success and be compared with benchmarks within a firm or for a sector.

To the extent that funds are available (which is becoming much less common in the public sector), managers who meet or exceed the desired standards or organizational benchmarks should be rewarded. Similarly, managers or groups who exceed production or service quality targets should be promoted as well. Natural resource organizations and professions, both commodity oriented and service oriented, have traditionally not been well-financed and high-paying sectors, which makes rewards difficult. Managers and leaders then must appeal to professional pride, altruism, scenic workplace benefits, and praise as tools to encourage employee loyalty, productivity, good customer service, and organizational success.

Continuous Improvement

The last step in a typical management cycle is to evaluate the success of an organization and identify areas for improvement, either periodically, annually, or over a longer term. Continuous improvement relates to the monitoring function just described but carries it farther to corporate or public organization outcomes in aggregate, not just for individuals. It includes systematic evaluation of success for an organization in achieving its goals. These can be measured within the organization over time and against outputs costs or profits for other firms in the same sector. Effective public organizations also require monitoring, evaluation, improvement, or termination of programs and policies as appropriate.

At a more micro level, individuals and different parts of a firm also can find and institute small continual improvements. These bottom-up management techniques and worker innovations are often promoted to help organizations improve processes and outputs at the grassroots level, where minor problems can be seen first and resolved quickly before they become major issues.

Organization of the Book

The following chapters in the book will discuss leadership principles, present short biographies of famous natural resource leaders for illustration, examine the unique context for natural resource leadership and professional careers, cover selected components of the management cycle shown in Figure 1.1, and present three cases from my experience as examples of more typical professional opportunities for leadership.

I start with an overview of various theories and principles of leadership, built around the theme from Block (2017) that leadership is aligning an organization's resources and actions with its stated intentions. That is followed by a short case study and biography of Jay N. (Ding) Darling, who epitomizes the career of an amateur naturalist—with wonderful insights and humor—who then became a leader and built enduring natural resource institutions. In addition, I discuss briefer cases of several modern leaders throughout the world and focus on their diversity and the breadth of the issues that they addressed to improve natural resources, social systems, and indeed existing human, animal, and plant life on earth.

After the examples of leaders, I cover the unique situation of leadership and management in natural resources in Chapter 4. The next chapter returns to management cycle and discusses most of its components and focuses on selected tools, strategies, tactics, and policies that can be helpful in leadership. Key tools that are required for effective leadership include having a clear vision and goals; proficient personnel management; open and transparent management and communication; fair and equitable treatment of employees, clients, and stakeholders; and monitoring and rewarding successful efforts.

Chapters 6 and 7 cover three cases that I have experienced as a leader at surely less globally significant levels but nonetheless important and challenging at local or national levels. These include cases on leadership and management as a federal research leader and as Department Head at a university, President of the SAF, and a conservation activist trying to stop the sale of our large university education and research Hofmann Forest. In sum,

I hope that these principles, cases, and examples provide an innovative mix of theory, literature, leaders, and comments that should be helpful for natural resource professionals in their jobs and careers. The last chapter briefly weaves together these principles, leadership cases, and personal examples to make conclusions about leadership and management practices for natural resource professionals.

References

Bendell J, Little R, Sutherland N. 2018. The seven unsustainabilities of mainstream leadership. In: Redekop BW, Gallagher DR, Satterwaite R, editors. *Innovation in Environmental Leadership*. London: Routledge. p. 13–31.

Block P. 1987. *The Empowered Manager: Positive Political Skills at Work*. San Francisco (CA): Jossey-Bass Publishers. 214 p.

Block P. 2017. *The Empowered Manager, Second Edition: Positive Political Skills at Work*. Hoboken (NJ): Wiley. 213 p.

Drucker P. 2001. *The Essential Drucker*. New York: HarperCollins.

Kotter JP. 1990. What leaders really do. In: *On Leadership*. Boston (MA): Harvard Business Review Press, 2011. Reprint R0111F. p. 37–56.

Morgan DF, Ingle MD, Shinn CW. 2019. *New Public Leadership: Making a Difference from Where We Sit*. New York: Routledge. 425 p.

Štreimikienė D, Mikalauskiene A, Ciegis R. 2020. *Sustainable Development, Leadership, and Innovations*. Boca Raton (FL): CRC Press. 267 p.

2 Natural Resource Leadership Principles

Defining Leadership

There is not a unified theory of leadership success for leaders and managers. There is considerable research and general agreement about leadership empowering workers and managers; treating people with respect; stressing the importance of mutual communication; identifying goals and objectives; developing effective policies and processes; balancing rules and flexibility; measuring, monitoring, and rewarding good performance; and encouraging diversity of opinions, culture, gender, and ethnicity in modern organizations. Leadership theory and texts usually recommend eschewing nefarious, duplicitous, or manipulative strategies, although they seem to occur too frequently in practice.

Aligning Actions and Resources with Stated Intentions

So as to not bury the lead, I will draw on a definition of leadership presented by Peter Block and then amplify that core vision by examining other literature in organizational management and natural resources. In the *Empowered Manager*, Block (2017) defined leadership:

> Leadership is the process of translating intentions into reality. If our intention is to work in an organization in which authority resides close to the bottom, within each person, and authenticity is the norm, then all we have to do is make sure that our own actions are aligned with our intentions . . . This is politics at its best, where our actions, not our speeches, become our political statement.
>
> (Block 2017, p. 97)

In brief, let me adapt this principle to state my definition that: **"Leadership consists of aligning an organization's actions and resources with its stated**

DOI: 10.4324/9781003141297-2

intentions." This infers that leaders and managers in any organization should align their personal actions, and commit the human and financial resources available, to the stated missions, vision, and goals of the organization. Of course, the reverse of this is true if any one of the preceding elements is foregone. Having missions and stated intentions that are vague or false, allocating resources to other priorities, or taking actions that do not fulfill the missions and vision will lead to poor performance. It is the job of good leaders and managers to perceive and articulate and be sincere in stating their vision and align what they say with what they do.

Each element of this definition is crucial. One's intentions, mission, and vision must be clear and accepted by an organization's leadership and by its employees. They must be reflected in an organization's objectives, rules, and policies. Furthermore, those stated intentions must be real, positive, actual goals that are desired, not fluffy or insincere statements designed for internal or external propaganda. Next, the labor and capital and management time and effort, as well as the actions the firm takes, must help achieve that mission and the stated intentions. And, similar to the management model displayed in Figure 1.1, the employee and organizational monitoring, evaluation, rewards, and continual improvement must seek to perfect these goals and processes. So the entire leadership and management cycle must strive for alignment between what an organization says and what it does.

The principle of aligning your vision, intentions, and actions over time is supported extensively in the management literature. For example, Covey (1990) states that leadership comprises four levels: (1) trustworthiness at the internal personal level; (2) trust among persons; (3) empowering people as a manager; and (4) aligning organizational actions and resources to achieve its goals. This marshals employees' talent to use their capacity, intelligence, creativity, and resourcefulness.

Aligning actions and resources with stated intentions is necessary for organizational success, but it is not sufficient by itself. There may be secret goals or hidden agendas in many organizations and actions or less transparent ways to achieve even clear goals. However, if either part of this principle is insincere—stated intentions are not real, or actions and resources are not aligned with real goals—an organization surely cannot achieve the phony goals or be successful if actions are misdirected. So in the long run, all the components of the preceding management cycle shown in Figure 1.1 must work in relative harmony, or organizations, leaders, managers, and employees will wander unproductively. In fact, Covey (1990) lists poor alignment between values, visions, and systems as one of his seven chronic problems of organizations.

Of course, aligning one's real intentions and resources and actions is by no means easy. Even if leaders perceive the correct goals for an organization, there may be varied actions that can be taken and various combinations of resources to commit to achieve those goals. Most organizations, products, and services will have multiple inputs and multiple outputs, and not one given path to success. There certainly will be tradeoffs in using one set of land, human, and financial resources versus another. This is particularly true with natural resources, which often encompass multiple outputs on the same area of land, some with market values and some without. Divining the best combination of equipment, personnel, land, and funds to achieve even clear goals is difficult. But at least starting with clear missions, visions, and statements of intent, and allocating resources in a manner that at least demonstrates sincere commitment, is a good start.

Despite the apparent merits of aligning missions, visions, and resources, Heifetz and Laurie (1997) argue that unilateral top-down visions and alignment treats problems as if they were technical and amenable to solution by an individual leader. In reality, most issues are complex and require adaptive management with the work and responsibility of managers and employees throughout the organization. Leaders from above or below, with or without authority, must confront organizational challenges, adjust their values, changing perspectives, and learn new habits. So, while visions and resources will need to be aligned, they are not fixed. Adaptive work requires that organizations identify changes in society, markets, customers, competition, and technologies and then clarify their values, develop new strategies, and learn new ways of operating. Leaders should take a big picture of the business environment; identify problems and issues collaboratively with employees; delegate work efforts back to employees; and protect outspoken voices from below, who can see problems first hand and provoke fresh thinking (Heifetz and Laurie 1997). In the complex world of natural resources and communities, these adaptive management approaches bear particular consideration.

Perception and Change

Leaders often perceive not only visions for organizations, but problems in particular. Except in unusual new organizations and new projects, a leader in an organization will seek to improve current visions, objectives, processes, manufacturing, service, or similar activities. Improvement or enhancement infers that existing status quo is not working well enough in some fashion. Leaders often have exceptional vision in both seeing and in articulating the big picture the long run, as well as setting a broad view of strategy and tactics needed for organizational success. This dual ability in fact helps individuals become leaders at many different levels in an organization or in their career path.

Very often current employees and managers can recognize issues and think of improvements, but they do not feel welcome to comment; are not empowered to act; feel that the issues are beyond their ability to change; think that the problems are not bad enough for intervention; or think they will be rebuked or yelled at for speaking up. Adaptive management is one approach to identify and resolve such problems and should be used by leaders to encourage the collective wisdom and contributions of all employees at all levels of an organization. Similarly, leaders who can open communication for input throughout an organization can help identify issues and solutions most effectively (Heifetz and Laurie 1997).

Leaders can meld their insights and employee views and input to develop a vison of what and how actions should be done and how it will benefit the organization. They have or take the authority to address problems, have the will and courage to bring them up, have ideas about what should be done to lead change, consult proactively with the diverse members throughout the organization to identify new objectives and approaches, and develop means to sell those changes to the rank and file who need to pursue a new vision.

Leaders often articulate and push and pull followers to do things that many people think do need to be done, but no one else is willing to lead. They often tell persons things that they sense, but do not want to hear or know, and have been avoiding studiously for a long time. Being popular does not equate with being a leader, and a love of praise prevents leadership effort. Leaders often may be challenging the status quo or vested interests in an organization or a community. They often may have to stand alone or with the support of only a few to fight for what they see and know is right. They may need to make decisions that cost them some relationships but will be better off making the right decisions and endure some criticism, letting time and good results prove them right (Tanner 2020).

Management literature also talks often about leaders as change agents or even as hiring change agents from the outside to reform poor practices and performance within organizations, from private businesses to public city managers to nonprofits and churches. In this case, the organizations generally recognize that they have problems but do not have internal capacity or will to lead, make tough decisions, and implement changes. This is an unfortunate state of affairs for both the incoming leaders and the recalcitrant existing managers, whose input and action may not always be welcomed. Nonetheless, talented and fortunate external leaders may be able to change organizations if needed but surely start with the disadvantage of broken systems when they start. Covey (1990) notes that a better approach is for organizations to be able to recognize issues from within; encourage open discussion; propose and adopt alternative solutions; and inculcate leaders, managers, and employees with the skills and tools and culture to break with traditional ways of thinking and create new paradigms to achieve their missions.

More Complexity

Despite its merits, having a single view of leadership misses the complexities of people and breadth of organizations. Addor (2010) summarizes a complex review by Bass (1990) that examines terms that characterize leadership, such as "influence relationships, power differentials, persuasion, influence on goal achievement, role differentiation, reinforcement, initiation of structure, and perceived attributions of behavior." In their tome on *New Public Leadership*, Morgan et al. (2019) list dozens of perspectives of leadership, each with numerous references. These include subsections on leadership as conciliatory practice leadership and as statecraft; leaders as managers of work structure and processes; leaders of managers and people; as managers of institutions; as managers of conflict and controversy; as creators and managers of culture; as Wicked Challenge management; and indeed as leading in aligning tasks with goals. In some sense, all these and other perspectives of leadership have merit. However, one can posit that real intentions, real actions, and real rewards surely are foundations for all other successful efforts or at least are intertwined throughout the workplace in order to achieve success.

In a trenchant book on contrarian leadership, State University of New York and University of Southern California president Steven Sample (2002) noted that leadership is full of minutiae, not just elegant visons and important personal interactions with important people. He posits a 70/30 formula that under ideal conditions, up to 30% of a leader's time can be spent on really substantive matters, such as independent thinking, planning, and inspiring their followers. No more than 70% of their time should be spent on reacting to or presiding over trivial, routine, or ephemeral matters. Distinguishing what is substantive from trivial is, of course, not easy, and trivial stuff may devolve into major problems if neglected. He also observes that a leader's substantive time may dwindle inexorably if not protected, so one must strive diligently to ensure that important leadership functions endure the onslaught of daily demands.

I might note that the lower one is in the leadership and management hierarchy, the more that the 70/30 formula degrades to a worse ratio, and one is fortunate to hold onto an 80/20 or even 90/10 share of dreck to substance. This unavoidable characteristic indeed is one major prompt for leaders to seek to move up to better positions or transfer to staff slots without line authority or back to technical positions—quickly if they find line management overwhelming or eventually if endless routine and often insoluble challenges wear them down.

At lower levels of management and leadership, persons also often try to hold onto some technical time and tasks in order to feel refreshed and productive in their jobs, making the 30% or so of the formula consisting of technical professional fun, if not resulting in leadership glory. They also might take temporary assignments in other jobs or locations, cross-train for other interesting skills, or take other actions that vary their jobs and tempo. Or they, of course, may compensate with hobbies, reading, arts and entertainment, sports, marathons, mountain climbing, or other more relaxing pursuits than middle management.

Classic Leadership Authors

While lofty statements about good or bad leaders are aspirational, finding empirical evidence is, of course, important. It is worth mentioning at least two classic authors and their findings about leadership and management to provide a broad and enduring context. I will briefly recap a couple of key articles from the *Harvard Business Review*. One is by Peter Drucker, perhaps the most famous expert on leadership and management in the United States, and Jim Collins, who followed slightly later, who is also universally well known. Both of these review articles provide an excellent foundation for understanding what makes good leaders, executives, and managers.

What Makes an Effective Executive

In a review article published first in 2004, and reprinted in a *Harvard Business Review* book in 2011, Peter Drucker summarized what made an executive effective based on his observations over a 65-year career. He notes that effectiveness does not have to be demonstrated by being a stereotypical leader. Drucker (2004) wrote that effective executives ranged widely "in terms of their personalities, attitudes, values, strengths, and weaknesses. They ranged from extroverted to nearly reclusive, from easy going to controlling, from generous to parsimonious."

All of the effective executives followed the same eight practices:

- "They asked, 'What needs to be done'?
- They asked, 'What is the right enterprise'?
- They developed action plans.
- They took responsibility for their decisions.
- They took responsibility for communicating.
- They were focused on opportunities rather than problems.

- They ran productive meetings.
- They thought and said 'we' rather than 'I'."

Drucker discussed each of these eight practices in detail; a few summary observations follow. Asking what needs to be done should focus on the organization, not what you want to do, and focusing what you do best first, and adjusting priorities as the most important tasks are resolved. Focusing on what's best for your enterprise is key and will lead to success for all owners, employees, investors, and customers. Success requires plans, actions, benchmarks, and revisions to achieve the desired results. Responsibility for decisions implies reviewing implementation, hires and promotions, and correcting poor decisions before they do real damage.

Per Drucker's practices, communication means getting input from superiors, subordinates, and peers and informing them about your plans. Interestingly, he advises focusing on exploiting opportunities, not solving problems, and using your best people to do so. He observes that problems must be solved, of course, to prevent damage, but exploiting change provides an opportunity for organizational success rather than a threat. In fact, changes such as technology, innovation, market demands, people's opinions, values, and business failures or successes could open new opportunities that can increase success if they are capitalized on rather than avoided.

In addition, meetings should be productive with a purpose; an agenda; closure, not rambling; and follow-up work assignments and deadlines. The most effective professional association committee chair that I served with followed this practice exactly and sent out minutes after every meeting with a list of discussion items, decisions, due dates for responses, and follow-up afterward. In addition, with each action memo, she included a subject line and a due date, so we knew the score and followed through. Importantly, Drucker also stressed that by working for the success of the organization, *we* must succeed together, not "*I*" the executive.

In the closing of his article, Drucker threw in a bonus practice, which was so important that he elevated it to the level of a rule: *"Listen first, speak last."* Drucker's rule is reflected by countless other observers of leadership. Sample (2002) notes that intensive active listening by drawing people out helps one learn additional details about an issue, as well as filters or biases of the speaker. Such listening also places a responsibility on the speaker to be careful and accountable. And the mutual communication helps clarify facts, values, and issues yet does not infer that the leader will take action, which should be deferred as long as possible until as much information as possible can be gathered from a variety of sources.

Sample (2002) also interestingly noted that leaders should have open communication and be free to listen and talk to anyone in their organization and perhaps to receive input from them at will. Indeed, a common adage for this is management by wandering around (MBWA). However, any commitments, allocations, and decisions should be made from the top down with structured decision-making through the hierarchy—the chain of command (Sample 2002).

Level 5 Success: Leadership Humility and Resolve

A seminal article by Jim Collins in 2001 in the *Harvard Business Review* concludes that the highest levels of leadership rest on humility and fierce resolve in leaders. Collins and his colleagues, of the *Good to Great* book fame, examined 1435 companies and measured which ones created the most wealth as measured by total stock market returns for 15 years. Of those, only 11 met their criterion of outperforming the stock market by more than four times the stock market average over those 15 years—which they termed as Level 5 leaders. These leaders were the antithesis of flamboyant. Collins (2001) gave the example of Darwin Smith, a mild-mannered in-house lawyer who became CEO at Kimberly-Clark Paper, who then led the company to phenomenal results for 20 years. He routinely credited others, external factors, and good luck for his company's success. If results were poor, he blamed himself.

Collins categorized employees, managers, and leaders into five hierarchical levels. Level 1 persons were highly capable, making productive contributions with talent, knowledge, and good work habits. Level 2 individuals contributed effectively as a team member in groups. Level 3 were competent managers who organized people and resources effectively and efficiently to achieve predetermined objectives. Level 4 leaders catalyzed commitment to a vigorous pursuit of a clear and compelling vision and stimulated a group to high performance standards. Level 5 leaders built enduring greatness with a paradoxical combination of personal humility and professional will (Collins 2001).

Level 5 leaders act quietly, calmly, and determinedly, relying on inspired standards, not insincere charisma, to motivate. Level 5 leaders never have a monumental ego or seek glory but instead sublimate their needs to those of sustainable success for their organization. Level 5 leaders focus on people first and strategy second; they get the best workers and managers possible and then figure out where to go. This does not mean that such leaders are not determined or eschew hard decisions of mission, major reorganization, change, strategy, hiring, evaluating, and firing people based on merit. Darwin Smith sold all the pulp and paper mills at Kimberly-Clark to focus on simply becoming the leading consumer paper products company in the world, competing against giants such as Scott Paper and Proctor and

Gamble (Collins 2001). In the political arena, Henry Waxman epitomized this approach as well. From 1985 to 2015, the remarkably uncharismatic Congressional Representative from California was probably a cosponsor of more legislation that was passed in health and the environment than any other and praised in 2021 by comedian Bill Maher as one of the star "work-horses" in Congress who led in passing bills on food safety, clean air, HIV research, and the social safety net.

Level 5 leaders also use what has been termed the "hedgehog concept"—determining what a company is best at, how its economics work best, and what ignites people's passions. Then they eliminate everything else. In addition, humble Level 5 leaders are not threatened by talent and try to seek and retain the best leaders throughout the organization, so that it will prosper when they leave, not just in the short term (Collins 2001). This example of the traits of the most successful CEOs in the United States for the 30 years from 1965 to 1995 provides empirical evidence that humility and resolve, not ego and aggression, lead best to long-term success. Level 5 leaders are ambitious, but they focus their ambition on the institution, not themselves (Gordon and Berry 2006). Level 5 leaders combine clarity of purpose and consistency of actions and resources with determined and demanding human resource and manufacturing management.

Shady Approaches and Consequences

While excellent leadership qualities are enduring, they are perhaps unusual as well. If they fail to align efforts with stated intentions and collaborate with managers, employees, and stakeholders, leaders and organizations will never fully succeed or reach their potential. False statements will either confuse or disenchant employees and muddle missions, produce skeptics, and cast doubt on all of the goals, merits, and good will of the organizations and leaders. Inconsistent statements, practices, and rewards can lead to disillusionment and cynicism. Savvy operators will recognize and respond to actual (unstated) organizational or leader's missions and rewards system and advance instead of those who play by the stated rules. Idealists will lose, satisfice, and reduce their loyalty.

Nonetheless, office politics do occur everywhere—in the private, public, or nonprofit sectors, as the moniker suggests. Of course, companies fail all the time, because of poor products and services, poor goals and objectives, poor processes, or indeed bad leaders and managers. Public agencies, government, and education, of course, have poor management at times as well but are less likely to be eliminated, although they may be reorganized periodically and have their leaders change often.

One can make a broad generalization that leaders should not be abusive, exploitive, intimidating, harassing, demeaning, scheming, manipulative, distrustful, or immoral. While such proscriptions are appealing, we all have had managers or experienced political leaders who have some if not all of these characteristics, and some have managed to advance to leadership positions, and at times had some success, or moved deftly on to other organizations to ply their dark arts. However, Covey (1990) notes that the use of manipulative strategies and tactics reflects a flawed character and questionable competency and can't lead to success over time. He adds that without trust, "there is no foundation for permanent success. But if we learn to manage things and lead people we will have the best bottom line because we will unleash the energy and talent of people" (Covey 1990, p. 17).

The Prince by Machiavelli (~1532), of course, epitomizes disingenuous strategies and tactics, based on a reputed, successful princes of politics and power in Italy. At least one of many such discouraging quotes for a prince bears note: "[S]omething which looks like virtue, if followed, would be his ruin; whilst something else, which looks like vice, yet followed brings him security and prosperity" (Machiavelli, version of 1908). However, while *the Prince* is famous, its impact in its era and perhaps since was modest and paled to vast long-term fame and impact of Erasmus in the same epoch. Erasmus was a paragon of liberal philosophy and morality and adviser to kings, princes, and priests throughout Europe for decades and advocated that leaders should be learned in philosophy, and should cultivate the habits of gentleness and public service, and helped foment humane and erudite modern civilization (The Economist 2020).

Let me also comment on the relative success of good and bad leaders. Being a good manager or a good leader per the definition adopted here or any other measures does not necessarily guarantee corporate, public agency, or personal success as measured by profits, advancement, pay, wealth, or other handy metrics. However, being a good leader by using straightforward goals, actions, empowerment, compassion, and rewards is more likely to lead to organizational and career success in the long run. On the other hand, greed, deceit, manipulation, coercion, intimidation, and frequent job changes may help one advance in a career for some period of time, and even a few CEOs were famous for abuse of power and terror. But most of them also fell to the earth and grounded their companies as well.

One example is perhaps worth retelling. One forest products firm in the 1990s had an infamously aggressive culture and at least one intimidating Vice-President who terrorized those who worked for him. Despite his ruthless management and creative efforts to sell timberland leases to make high quarterly returns, his entire timberland division was sold in a trend that swept the industry for two decades, and he was fired. Of course, all managers and leaders might mix ambition, talents, skills, honesty, misdirection, office politics, and power in varying degrees, but one might hope that openness, integrity, and fairness will produce better results for an individual and an organization.

Empowered Management

Aligning organizational resources and actions with stated intentions requires a broad set of leadership skills, approaches, and tools. Again, the management literature is voluminous regarding leadership approaches, so reviewing it all is not possible and not helpful for this primer. Per Colin Powell, leaders determine and provide a clear direction, so everyone stays on course. Determining such a course requires engagement of employees, feedback sessions, raw honesty, and patience as a leader. It also requires communication and an open atmosphere of opportunities, mutual respect, and responsibility (Coachwell 2017).

The Entrepreneurial Management Cycle

Figure 2.1 illustrates the concepts of organizational empowerment stated by Block (2017), who contrasts the bureaucratic cycle of management with the entrepreneurial and empowered cycle. Block spent most of a book elaborating on Figure 2.1; let me summarize key points drawn from its principles. A bureaucratic cycle stems from an authoritarian and dependent relationship for organizational management. There is a patriarchal contract between bosses and employees, where sycophants win, and independence is devalued. Employees serve their own interests or those of their bosses, not those of the organization. They manipulate situations to please the boss, are ingratiating, and are rewarded for their fealty. This, of course, does not lead to high productivity, open discussion, candor, identification of problems, nor innovation and solutions.

In contrast, in the entrepreneurial and empowered cycle, managers create a vision of greatness and delegate authority and decisions to employees to achieve that vision. Individuals are empowered to exercise individual authority, self-expression, and commitment to the vision. They act in their enlightened self-interest to achieve the vision. Self-interest for employees encompasses performing work that has meaning, providing service for the organization; acting with integrity; achieving impact with your work; and taking pride in mastery of the subject. Authentic tactics include honesty, sharing financial and production information and uncertainty; and using clear language that reflects reality (Block 2017).

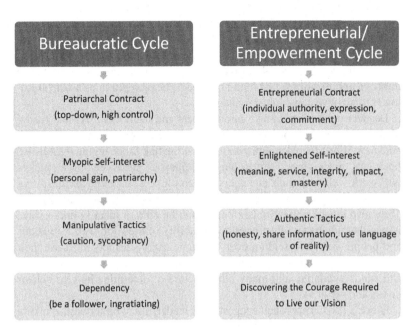

Figure 2.1 The empowered manager
Source: Adapted from Block 2017

These tactics parallel the four primary Covey principles (1990). Authentic tactics such as openness, rewards for merit, productivity, and honesty help employees and managers discover the courage required to practice the vision. Covey also observed that among his seven chronic organizational problems, lack of trust prevents communication, problem solving, and teamwork; and the lack of integrity creates lack of alignment in values and actions. The solution is, of course, the converse—instilling trust and open communication, and integrity and alignment of beliefs and actions.

Good leaders identify, affirm, or implement the vision of the organization. Leaders must create clear long-term and short-term visions in order to provide organizational cohesion and stability. Per Sample (2002), the greatest leaders throughout history have been the ones that could identify and recruit the best talent and marshal it effectively under a unifying vision. There is a temptation for leaders to choose individuals not quite as smart or good as they are, for fear of internal competition. But the long-term success of any organization demands that the leader not surround himself with yes-persons and sycophants (Sample 2002). They also need to encourage input, so they do not get isolated or unaware of issues that are harming their organization. Indeed, leaders must perceive or recognize visions and problems early, either individually or collaboratively. They also must pursue new actions to improve organizations, first, and not need to be dragged in as a fearful follower to achieve constructive changes.

Leaders must take input from customers and team members and recognize constraints and opportunities for their group or organization. They will lead new efforts to make improvements, taking flak for changing established practices, and giving credit to team members as deserved. Good leaders will work well with their managers and employees, listening and inspiring them to achieve the purposes, goals, and objectives of their organization. They also must be adept operationally and be able to identify and resolve issues that adversely affect employees' ability to their job well. Situations and people vary, and seldom does everyone agree. Leaders must use their assessment of a situation, the mission of their organization, the personnel and funds available, and many other factors to determine how to deliver goods and services.

Block's (2017) approach suggests that leaders must be forward-thinking and willing to act independently according to their values and conscience. Leaders must have a vision, be willing to learn and expand their idea of self-interest, engage in discourse authentically employing honesty and transparency, and be able to take action independently and courageously when it is not expedient. Leadership consists of pushing authority and responsibility to the lowest levels possible in an organization, where the most knowledgeable managers and employees can make decisions that achieve the organizational missions and objectives best.

Vision statements are, of course, tricky things, which often seem to consume an inordinate amount of time to develop and are not always followed well. However, good leaders will help develop and identify a useful vision or draw from existing statements and articulate them clearly and forcefully. Block (2017) states that visions should be clear, simple, and promoted frequently. They do not have to be profound but should be meaningful and useful.

Leaders must develop strategy and tactics to achieve a vision. They must listen and learn from staff and from customers. They must perceive and discern changes that can improve products and services, locally and regionally, and lead new efforts to make improvements. Leaders will both use existing organizational rules, procedures, and policies to achieve vision and create new ones that are needed to implement that vision. Leaders must follow rules but not let rules stymie action. They should use all the legitimate processes available for their actions, within the limits of good sense, personnel management, and ethics. Leaders must lead action to implement policies or to change policies and practices if they are unsuccessful, misguided, or immoral.

Implementation and Natural Resources

Evans et al. (2015) dissect the state of leadership research in environmental sciences based on an extensive review, starting with 850 references and yielding 187 relevant papers. They found that the literature classified leadership in terms of individual leaders or as sets of competencies. Example strategies of successful leaders in environmental sciences included visioning, knowledge building, innovation and learning, communicating, trust building, conflict management, macro- to detail-level thinking, and linking actors and stakeholders. Successful leaders' styles included adaptive, collaborative, democratic, political, process-oriented, system thinking, servant, transformational, and visionary components. They did not advocate any one of these particular approaches, but the list is an excellent overview of important leadership components.

Given such diversity of leadership components, leaders could follow the principles championed by Block and operationalize them in various ways. First, one should openly identify and state a vision and real intentions. This would include being clear about what the organization's primary products or service activities are. Then one can collaborate with the management team, employees, stakeholders, and customers to clarify and achieve the mission for producing goods or delivering services. Managers and leaders should allocate and adjust resources to achieve that intention. They should assign personnel and budgets based on benefits to mission. Leaders should make good work, team, and committee assignments. These assignments would need to recognize the constraints and opportunities with the tasks to be done and select the right personnel to carry them out.

Power, pay, perks, sycophancy, and flattery can outweigh sterling mission statements if leaders do not enforce norms to achieve the stated intentions. Flattery in particular may be more effective than imagined. Leaders often do feel beleaguered with making tough calls such as personnel issues, management tradeoffs between quantity and quality, or command and control versus autonomy. Charming and agreeable princes are far more apt to be appreciated than constructive critics. Modern examples where sycophancy and fealty led to ruin for modern companies included Enron, whose financial shams led to dissolution.

O'Farrell (2012) relates that the culture in AIG Financial (including VALIC), a key player in the financial crisis in 2007, was a dictatorship, where obedience and control were required values. She notes that Enron stated that integrity was a key company value but engaged in a web of creative accounting and deceit that led to its destruction. She does caution, however, that obsessive pursuit of any value or virtue can become a weakness. Too much honesty can be bluntness, perfection can lead to excessive control, and compulsive safety can lead to risk aversion.

Even in firms with excellent records, management can go awry. General Electric degenerated from brilliance to disaster due to dubious accounting practices to boost profits, focus on financial services instead of its core manufacturing legacy, and excessive hype (Schumpeter 2020). The rush to produce the Boeing 737 Max led to two crashes with 346 people killed. Reportedly, leaders cut costs to the bone and rushed the imperfect product to market, forsaking safety for profit. News reports and emails released in January 2020 stated that some workers refused to let their family travel on 737 Max. Two emails stated that "I still haven't been forgiven by God for covering up (what) I did last year," and "This airplane is designed by clowns who in turn are supervised by monkeys." In response, managers unfortunately stated that the employees who complained may be disciplined for the emails (Johnsson and Beene 2020).

The more the difference that exists between an organization's stated missions and values and the reality of what is pursued and who gets rewarded, the greater the performance problems will be. Organizational lack of trust will make everything within an organization harder. The longer the disparity between stated and real values occurs, the more wary employees become, the less credible senior management appears, and the worse organizational performance becomes (O'Farrell 2012). If organizations wander astray, leaders should (re)align their statements, values, resources, and actions. This should improve individual and corporate performance, internal good will, and the bottom line of profits for private firms or efficiency for public and NGO organizations.

References

Addor ML. 2010. An interpretative inquiry into natural resources and environmental leadership: Understanding the nature of a leadership development experience [dissertation]. [Raleigh (NC)]: North Carolina State University. 308 p.

Bass B. 1990. *Bass and Stogdill's Handbook of Leadership: Theory, Research, and Managerial Applications* (3rd Ed.). New York: The Free Press.

Block P. 2017. *The Empowered Manager, Second Edition: Positive Political Skills at Work.* Hoboken (NJ): Wiley. 213 p.

Coachwell [Internet]. 2017. Simplicity in leadership. Available at: www.coachwell.com/simplicity-in-leadership/. Accessed 14 February 2021.

Collins J. 2001. Level 5 leadership—The triumph of humility and fierce resolve. In: *On Leadership*. Boston (MA): Harvard Business Review Press, 2011. Reprint R0507M. p. 115–136.

Covey SR. 1990. *Principle-Centered Leadership*. New York: Free Press. 335 p.

Drucker P. 2004. What makes an effective leader. In: *On Leadership*. Boston (MA): Harvard Business Review Press, 2011. Reprint R0406C. p. 23–36.

Evans LS, Hicks CC, Cohen PJ, Case P, Prideaux M, and Mills DJ. 2015. Understanding leadership in the environmental sciences. *Ecology and Society* 20(1):50.

Gordon JC, Berry JK. 2006. *Environmental Leadership Equals Essential Leadership: Redefining Who Leads and How*. New Haven (CT) Yale University Press. 164 p.

Heifetz RA, Laurie DL. 1997. The work of leadership. In: *On Leadership*. Boston (MA): Harvard Business Review Press, 2011. Reprint R0111K. p. 57–78.

Johnsson J, Beene R. 2020. "Designed by clowns . . . supervised by monkeys:" Internal Boeing messages slam 737 Max. Bloomberg/Fortune. January 10, 2020. Availableat:https://fortune.com/2020/01/10/designed-clowns-supervised-monkeys-internal-boeing-messages-slam-737-max/. Accessed 25 May 2021.

Machiavelli N. 1908. *The Prince*. Translated by MK Mariott. London: JM Dent (Original); Reprint, Coppell (TX): Amazon. 87 p. ISBN-13: 978–15480 70687

Morgan DF, Ingle MD, Shinn CW. 2019. New Public Leadership: Making a Difference from Where We Sit. New York (NY): Routledge. 425 p..

O'Farrell I. 2012. *Values-Not Just for the Office Wall Plaque*. Dublin, Ireland: Evolution Consulting. 187 p.

Sample SB. 2002. *The Contrarian's Guide to Leadership*. San Francisco (CA): Josey-Bass. 197 p.

Schumpeter J. 2020. A GE whodunit. *The Economist* 436(9205):54. August 1, 2020.

Tanner R. 2020. Revisiting Colin Powell's 13 rules of leadership. *Management is a Journey*. Available at: https://managementisajourney.com/revisiting-colin-powells-13-rules-of-leadership/. Accessed 14 February 2021.

The Economist. 2020. Citizen of the world. 437:62–64. December 19, 2020. Available at: www.economist.com/christmas-specials/2020/12/16/erasmuss-teachings-are-still-pertinent-today. Accessed 25 May 2021.

3   Conservation Leaders from Ding Darling to Greta Thunberg

Introduction

It is useful to have examples of natural resource leaders whom we can emulate as professionals or as activists. In general, most professionals will be serving as leaders at lower to middle levels of their organizations and are not apt to be CEOs, Pulitzer or Nobel Prize winners, presidents, or environmental activists. However, some individuals who have achieved fame can serve as models of how one succeeds in traditional organizations or challenges the status quo to achieve transitory or enduring change to enhance conservation. The review in this chapter for Jay N. "Ding" Darling provides a brief biography, a recap of some of his notable management precepts and advances, and some relevant challenges that he faced in his career.

This chapter also presents short reviews of a few natural resource leaders appropriate for the modern era. The point in these biographies is to identify some key individuals and see how their values, technocratic professional training, and conservation principles interacted and how they influenced national or global natural resource management. These brief, tangible examples include famous persons to be sure, including Nobel and Pulitzer prize winners, but each leader had humble beginnings and kept their humility and compassion throughout their careers. In aggregate, they help illustrate a diverse and evolving set of examples of leadership in natural resources. The selections also help illustrate how the natural resource profession has expanded, both in its breadth of subjects it covers and in the diversity of the leaders in our field.

For brevity, the biographical reviews here begin at the start of the 20th century. After about a century of natural resource exploitation and Native American expropriation in the 1800s, new professional and technocratic conservation leaders of the Progressive Era emerged in the United States in the 1900s, most notably Theodore Roosevelt and cadre of new conservation advocates. Before he stepped down as President in 1908, TR had reserved

DOI: 10.4324/9781003141297-3

about 235 million acres (almost 100 million ha) of public land, either as National Forests, National Parks, National Wildlife Refuges, or National Monuments, and helped Congress establish new public land management agencies (USDI 2020).

Several famous persons cooperated closely with President Roosevelt—many of these in what was termed the "Conservation Cabinet." These include notables such as the first U.S. citizen trained as a forester, albeit in Nancy, France, Gifford Pinchot. Pinchot became the first Chief of the National Forests when they were transferred in 1905 from the U.S. Department of Interior to the Department of Agriculture. Pinchot promoted a utilitarian view of the use of forests for timber, range, and local communities, albeit under national management control. John Wesley Powell also served with TR and later became the head of the Bureau of Reclamation that built and managed dams in U.S. West, in part to fulfill Powell's vision of "making the desert bloom like a rose" (Cubbage et al. 2017). After that initial era of strong presidential leadership and public support, conservation expanded steadily throughout the 1910s and beyond.

Stephen Mather, the first director of the U.S. National Park System, which was created in 1916, also emerged as a conservation leader and promoted development of the parks to attract people and funding. Interestingly, the mission of the National Park System was one of the first to recognize and state today's version of sustainable development: "to conserve the scenery of the natural and historic objects and the wildlife therein and to provide for the enjoyment of the same in such a manner and by such means as will leave them unimpaired for future generations." The bifurcated mission's merits of conservation and providing enjoyment (recreation), however, were also a handicap at coalescing a solid constituent base (Clarke and McCool 1985), perhaps also a cautionary tale for sustainable development.

Ding Darling

Jay Norwood (Ding) Darling, who lived from 1876 to 1962, was part of the second wave of U.S. conservation leaders. He was a naturalist, political cartoonist, wildlife artist, conservationist, government administrator, and builder of several enduring U.S. wildlife conservation programs. Darling was born in Norwood, Wisconsin, as a child of a Congregational minister. His family moved to Elkhart, Indiana, and then Sioux City, Iowa, when he was 10. Darling spent much of his childhood there for a decade on banks of the Missouri River, exploring the expansive prairies of adjacent Nebraska and South Dakota and learning to view them as an ecological system. As soon as he was old enough, he worked to help herd cattle across the South Dakota plains (Lendt 1978).

Darling attended Beloit College as a biology major, where he penned his first satirical cartoons for the college yearbook, of the Beloit faculty, which he signed with his pen name of Ding for some anonymity. His irreverent caricatures (FWS.gov 2021) or his poor grades (Biographical Dictionary of Iowa 2021) earned him one of several suspensions, so he graduated 1 year late, in 1900. Nonetheless, at Beloit, a professor instilled the principle about the interdependence of all living things, which influenced Darling for the remainder of his life (Biographical Dictionary of Iowa 2021).

Political Cartoons and Conservation Causes

Darling intended to attend medical school and began working for the Sioux City Journal to save money. He started as a photographer but gravitated to political cartoons as his self-taught talents crystalized. He was hired to pen political cartoons for the Des Moines Register and Leader in 1906—in an era when the cartoons ran front and center on the front page of the newspaper. He excelled in cartoons covering conservation and politics, eventually promoting wildlife conservation and management throughout the United States (Goble et al. 2005). Like most leaders, Ding had the vision to see what was, and what could be, as well as unique talent to pen humorous and provocative cartoons that captured these issues and opportunities for publication throughout the country.

A cartoon by Ding aptly captures the interaction between good land stewardship and prosperity versus depleted soils, farms, and destitute families; and the challenge of government intervention, which he pursued throughout his career (Figure 3.1). Darling was hired by the *New York Globe* in 1911 but left unhappy because the *Globe* wanted him to pen cartoons more consistent with their political views than his.

Darling returned from New York—with invaluable contacts—to the *Register* in 1913, became syndicated by the *New York Herald Tribune* in 1916, expanded his adoption up to 130 daily newspapers, and won the first of two Pulitzer Prizes for political cartoons in 1924 (Biographical Dictionary of Iowa 2021). He purchased and renovated a grand house in the best neighborhood (Terrace Hill) in Des Moines, adjacent to the Iowa Governor's mansion and overlooking another river, the Raccoon. Darling then became active in Iowa conservation efforts and Republican politics. He stayed there most of his life, raising a son and daughter with his wife Genevieve Pendleton. They made periodic trips to their winter retreat in Sanibel Island, Florida.

Figure 3.1 As land goes, so goes man

Source: "Ding" Darling Wildlife Society owns the copyright of "Ding" Darling cartoons.

Building Conservation Institutions

Building on his national reputation, Ding devoted more of his career to conservation of natural resources, using his sharp perceptions, conservation principles, candid nature, and national contacts to help build wildlife and conservation institutions. These included organizing an Iowa Division of the Izaak Walton League—hunters, fishers, and conservationists. He served on the Iowa Fish and Game Commission starting in 1931 and started the nation's first Cooperative Wildlife Research Unit at Iowa State College (now University). Putting his money where his mouth was, he even personally contributed $3000 as matching to get the legislature to start funding the research unit. While that sum sounds modest today, it was enough to buy a 100 acre farm in 1931. The cooperative research unit became the model for U.S. Fish and Wildlife Cooperative Research Units that are now located at many universities throughout the country (Lendt 1978).

Darling was a staunch Republican and friend of fellow Iowan and ill-fated President Herbert Hoover but served on Democratic President Franklin Roosevelt's 1934 Committee for Wildlife Restoration, with famous wildlife experts and colleagues Aldo Leopold and Thomas Beck. He reluctantly agreed to become head of the dispirited federal Biological Survey in 1935 (now the U.S. Fish and Wildlife Service) and renewed its mission and vigor. In his brief 18 months there, he earned the moniker of "the best friend a duck ever had" and led the passage of the Duck Stamp Act, as well as designed the first stamp (FWS 2021). These stamps still are required for a federal permit to hunt ducks, and the artists who draw the winning stamp in the annual competition earn considerable fame for the rest of their careers.

After the brief stint with the Biological Survey, Darling helped found the National Wildlife Federation, now the largest citizen conservation nongovernment organization (NGO) in the United States, and served as its president for its first 3 years (Biographical Dictionary of Iowa 2021). He also worked with the League of Women Voters on wildlife education programs in the 1930s and 1940s. Darling also helped save his Florida home of Sanibel Island from massive development by getting part of the island declared as a national wildlife refuge (Lendt 1978), although much of the rest of the island and neighboring Captiva Island have been developed with expensive homes and condominiums.

Return to Politics, Conservation, and Cartoons in Iowa

Despite unparalleled success in his era, Darling eventually split from the National Wildlife Federation and with the League of Women Voters for becoming too materialistic and commercial in his opinion. He tried forming a new organization called Friends of the Land, but it eventually failed, to his great disappointment. He returned to Iowa from Washington, DC, in the 1940s and won another Pulitzer Prize in 1942. By the end of World War II, he helped organize better Iowa Republican Party efforts and opposed Presidents Roosevelt and Truman and even went so far as to praise Stalin's repressive but disciplined regime and criticize Roosevelt's Democratic Party idealism at the end of World War II. In addition, he opposed the national trend of more social legislation and international policy (Lendt 1978).

Nonetheless, Darling still fought for professionalism, not politics, in the Fish and Wildlife Service and the Iowa Conservation Commission. And far ahead of his time, he perceived that the toxic pesticide DDT could be a menace as great as an atom bomb and fought to have Iowa address the issue of falling water tables and have farmers and business pay for the efforts, not just the state. In particular, he also foresightedly opposed wasteful major projects such Red Rock Dam near Des Moines, saying that it would be better to stop runoff with small projects, which would "have the triple benefit of flood control, soil conservation, and restocking of our subterranean water table" (Lendt 1978, p. 260). He continued to fight for conservation until he died but with more rancor and less humor and hope than as a youth. For example, he "suggested that he was losing his knack for making a 'gripe sound funny'" (Lendt 1978, p. 260). His insights remain salient, his foresight about DDT was right, and small-scale local water and flood control projects are now becoming widely promoted as possible Nature-Based Solutions (NBS) that could replace large dams and levees.

The evolution of Ding as a leader and statesperson bears a quick note. In his first six decades of his life, he achieved unmatched success and awards as a political cartoonist, conservationist, administrator, NGO creator, and leader. In his later two decades, he remained active, insightful, and influential and won many national and international awards (Nielsen 2017). However, he became less sanguine about the directions of the country and conservation, more active but less successful in participating in politics, and less discerning about what conservation issues and battles to fight successfully and where the country was headed (Lendt 1978).

Overall, Ding's career of pragmatic productivity and diverse institution building was perhaps unequaled in his era. His insightful and funny political cartoons promoted and expanded the conservation movement throughout the nation. The Fish and Wildlife Service grew out of Biological Survey reforms that he instituted while Head. The National Wildlife Federation became the largest conservation NGO in the world, the Fish and Wildlife Cooperative Research units have expanded across the country, and the Duck Stamp remains the iconic face of waterfowl conservation and wildlife artistry to this day. Eventually, age, substantial ailments, and less good cheer diminished his efforts and influence, and perhaps his vision and pioneering conservation ideas were actually too far ahead of his time. And there is nothing wrong with that. Leaders cannot lead forever, but hopefully they will help build enduring organizations, as Darling did, while training and inspiring new followers and leaders.

Diverse Leaders for the Modern Era

While Darling led national efforts to promote wildlife conservation in the United States for a half century, a series of diverse leaders since have expanded the purview of such efforts in natural resource management in modern times. I cover several modern conservation and environmental leaders who provide tangible examples of leadership, as well as diversity, in our era. These start with David Attenborough of England and progress to Wangari Maathai of Kenya, a leader for forests and women's rights, and Marina Silva, an environmentalist and politician from Brazil. And youth will be served in environmental leadership—most notably, Greta Thunberg of Sweden, *Time*'s Person of the Year in 2019, who was 16 at that time. I also discuss Bob Brown from Australia, a renowned activist and politician, and Christina Koch, a young astronaut from North Carolina. These leaders demonstrate how natural resource leadership and diverse leaders have evolved in the modern era.

A Great Naturalist—David Attenborough

An exceptional leader of the newer generation of wildlife and environmental leaders is David Attenborough. Like Darling, Attenborough was a naturalist with brilliant media skills—only using the new broadcasting power of television in this case. Attenborough was born in 1926 and spent much of his childhood in Leicester, England, being fascinated by animals under rocks and the natural world (Attenborough 2020). He studied zoology at Cambridge, worked briefly in publishing, and then took a job as a junior television producer at BBC. Then in 1953, the 26-year-old Attenborough had a rare opportunity to film a series eventually named Zoo Quest for BBC. He began cooperating with BBC and Jack Lester, the London Zoo's curator of reptiles, to hunt rare animals and eventually ecosystems, but not to bring them back for zoos, but to film them in their habitats and dramatize their stories. Attenborough grasped that they needed to dramatize a quest for a rare animal in different continents to popularize the series. Lester and Attenborough went first to the jungles of the Sierra Leone seeking the rare *Picathartes gymnocephalus* bird and filmed the first pictures of the birds, as well as a wealth of small reptiles and insects (instead of megafauna of monkeys or antelopes) which could be moved and filmed in adequate light.

Lester, however, fell ill on the return from Africa. Lester recovered, and the team went off to British Guiana (now Guyana) in northern South

America, but he fell ill soon after arrival there. So Attenborough stepped in to become the lead naturalist, and fame followed. The team collected and filmed animals in situ, but only for filming, not for export back to zoos. Attenborough led a third major expedition to film the Komodo dragon in Indonesia. This was the largest lizard in the world but had never been seen on television (Attenborough 2017). The team then went to Paraguay, and the rest, as they say, is history. Attenborough became the iconic creator of Zoo Quest on BBC, which extolled the natural world. As the show matured, Attenborough led its modern production of the Blue Planet II, the most-watched nature documentary of all time.

Throughout his career, the naturalist used his insights, good fortune, talents, organizational skills, and media savvy to become the most revered chronicler of wildlife throughout the world. Indeed he has even been voted as the most popular person in Great Britain (Barkham 2019). The conservation media effects from Planet Earth 2 were examined by Fernández-Bellon and Kane (2019) by analyzing Twitter and Wikipedia hits. They found that natural history films can cause lasting connections and shifts in audience awareness, which are key factors for changing environmental attitudes.

However, like all leaders, even Attenborough has detractors. A few experts noted that in his recent Seven Worlds, One Planet, footage of a rare Andean bear from Ecuador was dubbed with the more common bear sounds. The South America episode also featured the sound of red-legged serie-mas, which are not found in the country or the reserve where the sequence was filmed (Collins 2019). Others criticize his failure to speak against the obvious detrimental impacts of humans causing mass extinctions, or about climate change, perhaps for commercial reasons. Some have criticized his grand oak dominance of the BBC nature landscape, with no heirs apparent being groomed, or even sought (Barkham 2019). At the age of 94, Attenborough (2020) may well have tried to redress these criticisms in his biopic *A Life on Our Planet*, which recognizes dreadful human impacts and climate change on the earth and calls us to restore global biodiversity and stability.

Women, Forests, and People

Other recent leaders of environmental movements certainly have led the fight to protect the pristine natural world that Attenborough documented so famously. Foremost among these have been two brave women who have led opposition to forest exploitation and development in Africa and Brazil—Wangari Maathai and Marina Silva, respectively. Both fought and led various efforts to protect forests, the environment, and women's rights, including halting deforestation, planting fruit trees, organizing women, building tree nursey capability, leading national involvement in politics and government, and more.

Wangari Maathai—In Africa, Professor Wangari Maathai (1940–2011) became a continental superstar, ecologist, and the first African woman to win a Nobel Peace Prize. She led environmental, human, and women's rights in her home of Kenya—efforts that spread throughout the continent. Maathai went from being a small village farm girl to be the first woman in east and central Africa to earn a PhD in biological sciences, from the University of Kansas. She became a professor and an activist fighting against environmental degradation in Kenya, as well as calling to halt global climate change.

In a retrospective speech presented at the United Nations, Maathai (2011) noted that while exploitation occurred throughout the world, it usually involved deforestation for exports to the developed world and that the world should commit to reform, and provide assistance to poorer counties. She observed that Africa is one of the poorest regions in the world, while it indeed is one of the richest in resources. But Africa needed better leaders to create the political environment that would unleash the energy of the African people and to participate in development and wealth creation.

In her fight against deforestation for forests and parks in her native Kenya and in Uganda, she faced powerful exploitive interests and dismissive national government leaders, led protests to protect parks, was jailed for her opposition, and lost her job as a professor (Nielsen 2017). In response, she formed her own organization and helped develop local capacity, practical knowledge, fruit tree nurseries, women's technical training in tree planting and tending, community service, and advocacy in the Green Belt Movement, which has now planted more than 40 million fruit and farm trees on community lands, including farms, schools, and churches (Development 2012).

To quote one memorial after she died of cancer in 2011 (Development 2012):

> She led the fight among communities, and nationally, running for parliament, and internationally as a leading participant of many international networks. She fought against poverty as the result of poor governance, environmental degradation and inequalities of the global economic system, as well as a deep gender bias that excluded giants like Wangari from the mainstream development processes.

Maathai was an ultimate activist, as inferred by the title of her book *Unbowed* (Maathai 2007). Such a life of activism may win admiration and friendships and impacts from common people to global statespersons, but it also may earn enduring enmity from vested interests who seek commercial gain, power, and domination. Nonetheless, Maathai was the epitome of courage, determination, and good cheer. In virtually every picture of her to be found, except when facing down forest guards who tried to stop her from planting trees, Maathai has the largest smile on the planet. Activism to help the environment, women, and communities surely agreed with her. Another memorial captures the spirit and price of such activism (Mulera 2011):

> "Where the world saw a woman who not only stood for justice and freedom for all Kenyans, but also spoke common sense in defence of our fragile planet, then President Daniel Arap Moi and his acolytes saw a "crazy woman" who was infested with "insects in her head." . . .
>
> I hold in high esteem those who believe in things beyond their stomachs, and have the courage to speak the truth even at the risk of losing friendships, opportunities and even their freedom or worse. Those who dispense with the hypocritical silence that enables many to eat with the powerful folks they privately despise, or even oppose find great favour in my estimation.
>
> To challenge a conservative culture that despised and exploited women was to act out one's beliefs without certainty about outcome. To do so in a society without the democratic institutional protection of one's freedom was supremely courageous. Then again Maathai would not have had it otherwise. Everything about her spoke of a sincere commitment to her beliefs, regardless of the painful consequences.

It also is worth mentioning that while Maathai risked her life to protect her forests and communities, many others have indeed given theirs to prevent deforestation and illegal logging, seek land reform, and protect indigenous rights. Birmingham and LeQuire (2010) list 19 persons, including 10 priests and one woman, who gave everything to be modern green heroes. Five of those persons, as well as Chico Mendes, leader of the Rubber Tapper Association, were in Brazil. These murders are truly a cautionary tale for persons who advocate for forests, land, locals, and indigenous rights.

Marina Silva—Following that caution, it is worth discussing the environmental leadership of Marina Silva, starting in the dangerous Amazon forests in Brazil. Silva was born in 1958 in the state of Acre in the Amazon, in a community of rubber tappers. She spent her childhood making rubber, hunting, and fishing to help support her large family. She was illiterate until she was 16 but soon earned a college degree at the Federal University of Acre. Growing from her background and education, she then cooperated with equally famous rubber tapper Chico Mendes to found the independent trade union movement in Acre (Goldman Prize 1996).

At that time, Acre was torn by an increase in deforestation and the invasion of indigenous and rubber tappers' land. In response, Mendes and Silva fomented peaceful demonstrations (*empates*) by forest-dwelling rubber tappers against deforestation and expulsion from their lands. These grassroots demonstrations helped protect thousands of hectares of tropical forests and the livelihoods of hundreds of rubber tapper families. Chico Mendes was assassinated in 1988, but Silva pressed on. Many more sustainable extractive reserves were established, now totaling more than 2 million hectares, managed by the traditional communities (Goldman Prize 1996).

In 1994, Silva was the first rubber tapper elected to Brazil's Senate, becoming the youngest Senator ever in Brazil. As a charismatic populist, she pushed for environmental protections for the Amazon, as well as social justice and sustainable development. She served in President Lula's administration as Brazil's environmental minister from 2003 to 2008 but resigned in protest of her lack of success in protecting Brazil's forests and environment. She then ran for the presidency in 2010 and 2014 with the goal of becoming, in her words, "the first black woman of poor origins" to win the job.

While not successful in her presidential candidacies, Silva remains an intellectual and spiritual leader, advocating for indigenous communities, sustainable development, better education, and women's equality. Her enduring vision has been "Brazil as a society that is economically successful yet respected in the world for its humanity and social consciousness" (Harvard Women's Law Association 2015). Despite her laudable accomplishments and goals, Brazil still has not been ready to forego development and transfer power to political advocates for greener forests, instead of cattle pastures. Silva's many successful efforts have been the first steps, but not the final story protecting communities, forests, and the environment throughout the country (Franco 2010).

Greta Thunberg and Climate Change

In current times, no environmental activist or leader is more famous than Greta Thunberg of Sweden. At the age of 15, Thunberg started her crusade in August 2018 with a simple one-person school strike on Fridays, in front of the Swedish Parliament, to protest global lack of action to prevent climate change. Her actions fomented similar school strikes throughout the world, as well as a new youth movement to prevent climate change. A year later, In September 2019, an estimated 7.6 million people from 125 countries as well as thousands of business, trade unions, universities, and other organizations participated in a Global Climate Strike (Martiskainen et al. 2020).

On September 23, 2019, Thunberg presented perhaps the most memorable environmental speech on record while speaking to a U.N. panel. The speech reflected her accumulated passion, extensive complex scientific details, anger, and persuasion to lambast pusillanimous politicians and shame the world into action in order to prevent impending doom from climate change. A partial quote from that 5-minute, riveting speech follows (NPR 2019):

> "This is all wrong. I shouldn't be up here. I should be back in school on the other side of the ocean. Yet you all come to us young people for hope. How dare you!"
>
> "You have stolen my dreams and my childhood with your empty words. And yet I'm one of the lucky ones. People are suffering. People are dying. Entire ecosystems are collapsing. We are in the beginning of a mass extinction, and all you can talk about is money and fairy tales of eternal economic growth. How dare you!"

There is a huge amount of popular literature and burgeoning scientific literature about Thunberg. In December 2019, Thunberg was declared the Person of the Year by *Time* magazine. Popular literature has millions of Google hits referring to her and the youth movement. She is extolled and trolled on the internet, and she continued her weekly strikes throughout 2021 as well.

These efforts follow a rich modern tradition of environmental movements and activism protesting adverse human impacts on ecosystems and the natural world. Climate protesters have varying ranges of knowledge about climate changes and have taken a variety of personal actions to reduce climate change (Martiskainen et al. 2020). Zulianello and Ceccobelli (2020) conclude that Thunberg's message is grounded in ecocentrism, technocracy, and scientific glorification, and a "Manichean" struggle between spiritual good and material evil. Sabherwal et al. (2021) conclude in their title that "[f]amiliarity with Greta Thunberg predicts intentions to engage in climate activism in the United States."

It will certainly be interesting to see how Thunberg, activists, scientists, politicians, and others work to build institutional change and how much can be achieved, or not, similar to her predecessors and others mentioned earlier. The black and white Manichean perspective certainly extends to views of Thunberg, who is glorified and reviled by persons from different sides. She is a hero and leader for many, along with her compatriots of very organized youth groups and activists. Conversely, she is so hated by opponents that even a mural of her in Dublin was defaced within two days of completion in March 2021. So certainly Thunberg is one of the greatest models of modern leadership and activist success, concomitant with all the merits and hazards that go with being a leader. Natural resource professionals surely aspire to less notoriety but still will be leading and waging smaller but challenging battles for constructive change in their organizations and for the sustainable management of their resources.

Closing Mention

There are many other great modern scientific and environmental leaders throughout the world, but covering them all could be an endless task for a brief book. For brevity, let me mention two more who demonstrate the character of leadership and how it has changed and become more diverse in the 2000s.

Bob Brown—Bob Brown is an environmentalist, human rights activist, and politician from Australia who also is a personification of modern leadership. His accomplishments and activism surely could fill a book by themselves. Brown was born in 1944 in New South Wales and moved to Tasmania in 1973. He obtained a medical degree in Sydney, served as a doctor in England, and returned to Australia. In his long career of activism and public service, he was a social justice and peace advocate, member of the Tasmania state parliament and Australian Senate, and the leader of the Australian Greens political party.

In 1976, Brown cofounded the Tasmanian Wilderness Society and led a campaign to save the Franklin River from a hydroelectric dam (Milne 2006). One major dam protest of more than 2,500 people led to his arrest and 19 days of incarceration. This was followed the next day with his release and appointment as a member of the Tasmanian Parliament, and he then won an election for that seat, as its first Green Party and openly gay member (Ray 2020). As leader of the Green Party, he helped lead the party to become a political force for three decades and led Australia to enact a carbon tax to take effect in 2012 to combat climate change. He fought successfully to rescind laws that could imprison persons for gay sex. And he was characterized at various times as visionary, dogmatic, courageous, humanitarian, an eco-warrior, and a power monger (AAP General News 2012).

While I always avoid Wikipedia and discourage its use by my students, the summary there is too good and other literature so sparse, I will make a risky exception (even *The Economist* praised Wikipedia in 2021). Their article notes that Bob Brown's advocacy and foresight as a legislator and an activist are stunning, sometimes with success and sometimes not. These have included advocacy to oppose the dam in Tasmania and to battle climate change, opposing wind turbines in order to protect native birds, opposing mining and selling coal for export, opposing logging of Tasmanian forests for wood chips, favoring regulation of semi-automatic weapons, and opposing Australian participation in the war in Iraq. These efforts generated virulent opposition from major firms and the government and expensive lawsuits against him that required that he pay for damages for his activism, as well as veneration for the passion, depth, and personal efforts and sacrifices he made for the causes he espoused (Wikipedia 2021).

Christina Hammock Koch—For one last hometown favorite of a diverse modern leader, let me briefly mention Christina Koch, as an excellent young NCSU role model. Koch is an astronaut, not a natural resource professional per se, but she has indeed worked in science and natural resources extensively, including two different stints in Antarctica, as well as being an outdoor enthusiast as a boater, rock climber, and photographer. Koch was born in 1979 and raised in Jacksonville, North Carolina, which is home to a Marine base, exposing her to people from all around the world. Koch received a BS and MS in Electrical Engineering at NC State University in 2001 and 2002.

Koch started with the U.S. National Air and Space Administration (NASA) in 2001 and progressed well there. However, despite its reputation, she did not stay on a single-minded track to be an astronaut and took risks and different jobs at various locations to expand her worldview, literally. Between her NASA career appointments, she went to the South Pole as a scientist in 2003 and 2010, had a job as an electrical engineer technician with Johns Hopkins University Applied Physics Lab in 2007, and then became an International Space Station Astronaut in 2013 (Murphy 2019). Then in March 2019, she completed 328 days in space, the longest stay of any female astronaut (Hajela and Murphy 2019).

Koch's career is remarkable, and her values contributed to that. In an interview with the *Raleigh News and Observer* newspaper, she noted that her multicultural experiences as a child helped form her success. She stated that "[It] made me realize that everyone can contribute together and that we work best when we are a diverse group working together." She added, "Those values of treating everyone well and putting people first are some of the things I still carry forward with me from North Carolina today." She recalled that her family had *National Geographic, Astronomy,* and *Popular Mechanics* magazines laying around the house, triggering her interest in exploration and different parts of the world and different parts of the universe (Murphy 2019). Again the mix of science, appreciation of diversity of people and of life experiences, and incredible effort makes Koch a leader and may offer her an opportunity to be the first woman on the moon.

References

AAP General News. 2012. Brown bows out, vowing to stay green. AAP General News Wire; Sydney [Sydney]. April 13, 2012. ProQuest document ID: 993966061.

Available at: https://proxying.lib.ncsu.edu/index.php/login?url=www.proquest.com/wirefeeds/fed-brown-bows-out-vowing-stay-green/docview/993966061/se-2?accountid=12725. Accessed 6 April 2021.

Attenborough D. 2017. *Adventures of a Young Naturalist: The Zoo Quest Expeditions, 2017 Edition*. Great Britain: Two Roads. 398 p.

Attenborough D. 2020. *A Life on Our Planet*. New York: Hachete Book Group. 266 p.

Barkham P. 2019. The real David Attenborough. *The Guardian*. October 22, 2019. Available at: www.theguardian.com/tv-and-radio/2019/oct/22/david-attenborough-climate-change-bbc. Accessed 6 March 2021.

Biographical Dictionary of Iowa. 2021. Darling, Jay Norwood "Ding." Available at: www.uipress.lib.uiowa.edu/bdi/DetailsPage.aspx?id=86. Accessed 20 January 2021.

Birmingham B, LeQuire SL. 2010. Green heroes reexamined: An evaluation of environmental role models. In: Redekop BW, editor. *Leadership for Environmental Sustainability*. New York: Routledge. p. 107–121.

Clarke JN, McCool D. 1985. *Staking Out the Terrain: Power Differences Among Natural Resource Agencies*. Albany: State University of New York Press. 198 p.

Collins J. 2019. BBC to pull parts of David Attenborough documentary after animal sounds mix-up. *Inews*. Available at: https://inews.co.uk/culture/bbc-to-pull-parts-of-david-attenborough-documentary-after-animal-sounds-mix-up-363944. Accessed 6 March 2021.

Cubbage F, O'Laughlin J, Peterson MN. 2017. *Natural Resource Policy*. Long Grove (IL): Waveland Press. 505 p.

Development. 2012. Last word: In memory of Wangari Maathai. *Development* 55(1):148–149. doi:10.1057/dev/2011.110.

Fernández-Bellon D, Kane A. 2019. Natural history films raise species awareness—A big data approach. *Conservation Letters* 13:1. doi:10.1111/conl.12678.

Fish and Wildlife Service (FWS). 2021. Jay Norwood "Ding" darling. Available at: https://fws.gov/refuges/hitory/bio/darling.html. Accessed 20 January 2021.

Franco LM. 2010. Brazil's green princess and presidential candidate Marina is no tree-hugging populist. *Brazil*. ProQuest Document Number 755280268. Accessed 25 August 2010.

Goble DD, Hirt P, Kilgore SJ. 2005. Environmental cartoons. *Environmental History* 10(4):776–792.

Goldman Prize. 1996. Marina Silva—1996 Goldman environmental prize recipient, South and Central America. Available at: www.goldmanprize.org/recipient/marina-silva/. Accessed 6 March 2021.

Hajela A, Murphy K. 2019. *Dream Achieved: NC State Grad Breaks Record for Longest Flight by a Woman*. Raleigh (NC): The News & Observer. December 28, 2019. Available at: www.newsobserver.com/news/local/article238777073.html. Accessed 6 March 2021.

Harvard Women's Law Association. 2015. Women inspiring change—Marina Silva. Available at: https://orgs.law.harvard.edu/womeninspiringchange/2015-honorees/marina-silva/. Accessed 5 March 2021.

Lendt DL. 1978. Ding: The life of Jay Norwood Darling. [retrospective dissertation 6464]. [Ames (IA)]: Iowa State University. Available at: https://lib.dr.iastate.edu/rtd/6464. Accessed 21 January 2021.

Maathai W. 2007. *Unbowed: A Memoir*. London: William Heinemann. 352 p.

Maathai W. 2011. Challenge for Africa. *Sustainability Science* 61:2. doi:10.1007/s11626-010-0120-2.

Martiskainen M, Axon S, Sovacool BK, Sareen S, Furszyfer Del Rio D, Axon K. 2020. Contextualizing climate justice activism: Knowledge, emotions, motivations, and actions among climate strikers in six cities. *Global Environmental Change* 65:120180. doi:10.1016/j.gloenvcha.2020.102180.

Milne C. 2006. *Bob Brown. The Companion to Tasmanian History*. Centre for Tasmanian Historical Studies. Available at: www.utas.edu.au/library/companion_to_tasmanian_history/B/Bob%20Brown.htm. Accessed 2 April 2021.

Mulera D. 2011. Prof. Wangari Maathai—Crazy Woman Unbowed [column]. *AllAfrica.com*. Washington (DC): ProQuest document ID: 1012119183.

Murphy K. 2019. Christina Koch, Tar Heel of the Month, explores from the International Space Station. Raleigh (NC): News & Observer. August 23, 2019. Available at: www.newsobserver.com/news/local/article234229227.html. Accessed 6 March 2021.

Nielsen L. 2017. *Nature's Allies*. Washington (DC): Island Press. 255 p.

NPR. 2019. Speech by Greta Thunberg at the United Nations Climate Action Summit, 23 September 2019. Available at: https://www.npr.org/2019/09/23/763452863/transcript-greta-thunbergs-speech-at-the-u-n-climate-action-summit. Accessed 6 March 2021.

Ray M. 2020. Bob Brown: Australian politician. Available at: www.britannica.com/biography/Bob-Brown. Accessed 2 April 2021.

Sabherwal A, Ballew MT, van der Linden S, et al. 2021. The Greta Thunberg effect: Familiarity with Greta Thunberg predicts intensions to engage in climate activism in the United States. *Journal of Applied Sociology/*Early view. doi:10.111/jsap.12737.

USDI. 2020. The conservation legacy of Theodore Roosevelt. U.S. Department of the Interior. Available at: www.doi.gov/blog/conservation-legacy-theodore-roosevelt. Accessed 25 May 2021.

Wikipedia. 2021. Bob Brown. Available at: https://en.wikipedia.org/wiki/Bob_Brown. Accessed 2 April 2021.

Zulianello M, Ceccobelli D. 2020. Don't call it climate populism: On Greta Thunberg's technocratic ecocentrism. *The Political Quarterly* 91:3. doi:10.1111/1467-923X.12858.

4 Natural Resource Context
Goods and Services, Professionals, and Careers

Work and Fulfillment

One basis for success in leadership and management is simply doing one's job conscientiously and well. Those who lack employment lament its absence and celebrate finding meaningful work. The massive unemployment of the Great Depression in the 1930s had rates of up to 25% of adult men without work—and did not even measure women as part of the workforce. Official U.S. unemployment then was redressed in part through creation of the Civilian Conservation Corps. That massive federal program was a model for offering worthwhile employment and modest incomes and helped imbue the nation with pride in government and in conservation for decades.

Personal fulfillment and rewards from work and employment are hardly new. Maslow (1943) originated the classic hierarchy of basic goals or needs, ranging from physiological, safety, love, esteem, and self-actualization. Many of these needs from the most basic food, shelter, and clothing to the highest goals of self-actualization are achieved either partially or largely through work, of course.

Stephen Covey (1990) provides profound insights about the meaning and value of work and of core natural principles that guide personal and organizational success. Principles include: "values, ideas, norms, and teachings that uplift, ennoble, fulfill, empower, and inspire people" (Covey 1990, p. 17). He expounds at length on relations between personal life centers and organizational life centers, where leadership and empowerment consist of treating people as you would want to be treated and that organizational leadership consists of explaining the principles that underly tasks (the why), not just the practices (the how). He observed that people are spiritual persons who want to do something that matters and has meaning.

DOI: 10.4324/9781003141297-4

Scores of years before Covey, Kahalil Gibran's (1923) poetic classic *The Prophet* extolled the spiritual virtue of work:

> You work that you may keep pace with the earth and the soul of the earth . . .
> When you work you fulfil a part of earth's furthest dream, assigned to you when that dream was born,
> And in keeping yourself with labour you are in truth loving life,
> And to love life through labour is to be intimate with life's inmost secret . . .
> Work is love made visible.

The value of work became even more obvious with its scarcity during the Covid-19 Coronavirus pandemic. Senator Marco Rubio (Rubio 2020) noted this insightfully in an article in *Time*:

> There is an inherent dignity that comes from work. I saw this as a child when I marched the picket line with my father . . . and it was foundational. . . [there is] an implicit understanding that there is no replacing the sense of dignity that comes with a paycheck and the ability to provide for your family.

The personal value of work extends into leadership, including emotional, ethical, and spiritual components. Covey (1990) observed that people want to pursue purposes that ennoble them and to contribute to the accomplishment of worthwhile objectives and transcend their individual tasks. Samul (2020) observes that the spiritual components of leadership tend to encourage individuals to make contributions beyond their own interests and contribute specifically to sustainability in the workplace.

In an extensive review of 373 articles on spirituality and leadership, Samul (2020, p. 6) observes that "[w]orkplace spirituality provides a suitable context for employees where they can feel a sense of meaningfulness and connection with others." She continues to write that personal spiritual leadership leads to organizational spiritual leadership, and then to sustainability— for example, the triple bottom line of ecological, social, and economic development. Furthermore, the integration of spiritual leadership in the workplace can reinforce the sustainability of that organization.

Spiritual rewards for employment in natural resources are particularly high. Almost all natural resource professionals entered the disciplines because they like nature, working outside, or dislike being cooped up in an office. Nature is, of course, the etymological and spiritual root for our love of natural resource disciplines. Whether it be parks and recreation, fish and wildlife, hunting, fishing, conservation biology, forest and range management, soils and watershed management, or related fields, we chose these professions as our passion, not just as our jobs. High pay and wealth are uncommon, and most natural resource professionals accept this rather than more lucrative career opportunities. Doing one's job well, then, becomes the basis for professional fulfillment. By recognizing the personal meaning in work, and seeking to excel in technical and relationship aspects of employment, one begins to grasp and practice leadership skills.

Private and Public Goods and Services

Natural resource management and leadership are somewhat unique in the types of market and nonmarket resources produced, managed, or protected, and the complexity of the private and public ownership and governance mechanisms that they require. Some natural resource lands and water produce private goods such as crops, fruits, timber, and fish, which are amenable to production and trade by individuals in markets. Natural resources also allow production of toll goods, which are consumed jointly, such as camping, climbing, concerts, boating, and some types of fishing, for which exclusion, restricted access, and charging for use are possible. Toll goods may be provided well by markets or may involve government provision, perhaps for a fee, depending on the situation and government land ownership or regulation.

Common pool goods, such as open range, marine fisheries, water, and air, are consumed individually, but it is difficult to exclude other users and charge fees. As a result, common pool goods may be consumed to the point of exhaustion or at least until the cost of extraction exceeds the utility for the individual. This is referred to as the classic tragedy of the commons (Hardin 1968), such as when grazers compete among themselves by stocking as many cattle as they can on unregulated public rangeland, leading to overgrazing and a destruction of the resource. Public control or allocation of common pool goods is typically advocated to ensure proper assignment of costs and socially acceptable levels of use. Collective goods are jointly consumed and not excludable, such as national defense, forest fire control, scenic vistas, or carbon storage. Common pool and collective goods are referred to broadly as public goods (Farley and Costanza 2002; Farley 2012).

The types of goods and services that the earth provides have been categorized by the Millennium Ecosystem Assessment (MEA 2005) into supporting, provisioning, regulating, and cultural services (Figure 4.1). *Supporting* services include nutrient cycling, soil formation, and primary production.

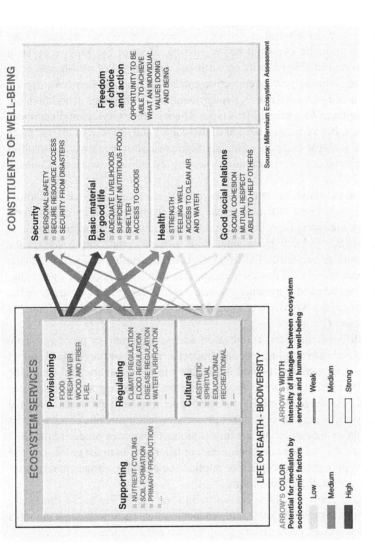

Figure 4.1 Ecosystem service schema from the Millennium Ecosystem Assessment (MEA 2005). Permission courtesy of World Resources Institute

Provisioning services include market commodities such as food, freshwater, wood and fiber, and fuel. *Regulating* services include climate regulation, flood regulation, disease regulation, and water purification. *Cultural* services include aesthetic, spiritual, educational, and recreational.

Some of MEA goods are largely private, which are provided relatively well by individuals and companies interacting in private markets, albeit with some public oversight and regulation. Most of the MEA ecosystem services and life/biodiversity on earth and constituents of well-being, however, are common pool or collective goods. These at the very least depend on the quality of governance, management, and leadership. In addition, not only are there four broad MEA types of ecosystem services and commodity goods, but very often several of these are jointly produced on one piece of land, with the prospect of having both positive or negative externalities for profits or environmental quality among the different services (Cubbage et al. 2017).

These extensive private market, public ecosystem service, and often shared governance systems are the relatively unique milieu that natural resource managers work in. At a minimum, a large share of natural resource lands are held publicly by national, state, local, or community governments. This includes one-third of all U.S. forest lands, one-third of all U.S. lands, and about 80% of all forests in the world. This share in public ownership, and of public goods, probably exceeds that in almost any other sector of the economy in the world, except possibly the oceans and air, which almost all are common pool goods.

While most industrial production and service market processes have some environmental impacts and tradeoffs, natural resource management has these impacts intertwined intrinsically in almost every decision made and action taken. Private firms and individuals produce goods and services with an exchange of money for the inputs into their production for the employees, managers, or capital (e.g., private factor markets), and a similar exchange of money (or barter) for the product or service produced (product markets). Private firms, entrepreneurs, or labor seek to make profits or good salaries, perhaps with explicit or implicit social and environmental responsibility as benefits or constraints.

Natural resource managers on private or public lands are producing some market goods in factor and product markets and surely large amounts of ecosystem services that they usually are not compensated for. Ecosystem services are closely related to public goods, comprising the ecological and natural resource set of public commodities, goods, and services. Their provision or protection requires action by governments; stewardship by private owners; or collective action by government, nongovernment, and private entities.

Wicked Problems

The challenge of public goods and public lands has been related to Rittel and Webbers's (1973) typology of tame and wicked problems (Grint 2010). A tame problem may be complicated but is resolvable through unilinear acts and is often recurring. A wicked problem is more complex and cannot be separated from the natural, social, or political environment and context that it occurs in, nor unilaterally solved by managers or routine actions (Grint 2010). Tame problems may be likened to management—solving existing or recurring problems that have occurred before—with advances in knowledge and technology. Wicked problems require leadership to identify, facilitate, and develop responses to often intractable problems, which often will continue without a definitive solution.

Natural resource management has grown to be characterized as a "wicked problem" that has no clearly identifiable solution and is part of a large set of different causes and influences and that does not have clear scientific or political solutions. Natural resources are not unique in this regard—professionals in public safety, education, social work, and more face similar situations, as well as substantial budget and personnel limitations (Morgan et al. 2019). Similar wicked problems and elusive solutions or best practices span issues such as poverty, racism, watershed management, wildlife restoration, and education.

Routine actions such as building campgrounds, making prescribed fire or habitat burns, developing a national wildlife refuge management plan, or making a profit growing timber are often not easy, but they are ongoing management actions that can be accomplished with professional expertise and adequate resources. Wicked problems that involve a large network of natural resources; the environment; social systems; private, government, and nongovernment organizations; uncertainty; economic impacts; and social values—such as climate change—are obviously extremely complex if not insoluble and will provide the basis for struggles and only small advances for generations.

Natural resource management problems are inherently complex and unique in space and time. Such problems do not have an agreed-upon body of knowledge or set of practices that will bridge competing political, ethical, or scientific claims. There is no uniformly agreed-upon public good, objective definition of equity, or specific correct or false answer. Such social and natural resource problems are not solved but rather recycled continually. Each implemented solution will leave traces that cannot be undone and will consume resources (financial and otherwise), which cannot be spent on another (Rittel and Webber 1973; Morgan et al. 2019). These problems are characterized by dynamic conditions, scientific complexity, multiple stakeholders with diverse and at times competing values and goals, and a lack of resources, time, and information (Lachapelle et al. 2003).

Natural resource managers in the public sector are not unique in facing wicked problems, but they certainly must adapt, manage, and lead in order to deal with this complex environment (Morgan et al. 2019). Leaders must learn to deal with problems ranging from simple to chaotic and understand what the issues are. Depending on the complexity and urgency, leaders must communicate among stakeholders, create teams of experts, and focus on key issues and problems. Most of this theory on tame or wicked problems occurs in the public administration literature. To quote Morgan et al. (2019, p. 221):

> Complicated problems represent the home of classic public administration, where the expertise of a specially trained cadre of professional career administrators is needed to sort, order, plan, coordinate, develop and implement solutions to challenges, both simple and complex, under the direction of elected officials.

The private sector is only considered as one of the stakeholders, interest groups, or partners in a complex natural resource situation. This perhaps infers that all private sector problems are tame, which is not accurate. To be sure, private companies, landowners, and individuals are part of most natural resource problems, even on public lands, and certainly on intermingled public and private lands. But even in private land ownerships, while natural resource management may be less complicated, wicked problems occur, and natural resource leaders are crucial.

Private natural resource landowners and NGOs need vision, leaders, and the ability to resolve intractable problems continually. In current times, companies must not only make profits but also demonstrate their environmental and social governance (ESG) and corporate social responsibility (CSR). Chen (2021) summarizes that ESG are criteria that socially conscious investors use to screen potential investments. He writes:

> Environmental criteria consider how a company performs as a steward of nature. Social criteria examine how it manages relationships with employees, suppliers, customers, and the communities where it operates. Governance deals with a company's leadership, executive pay, audits, internal controls, and shareholder rights.

Mutual funds and brokerage firms offer products that employ ESG criteria, and there also are various companies that evaluate ESG performance and sustainability. The application of such criteria and investment tools help guide investor's actions and substantially influence how private firms practice and demonstrate sustainability and responsibility. ESG standards can also help investors avoid companies that might pose a greater financial risk due to their poor environmental or other practices. CSR for the private sector efforts include organic food and voluntary environmental programs (VEPs) such as seafood and forest certification programs.

Private landowners also must deal with commodity production and services (e.g., timber, hunting leases), environmental protection (e.g., wildlife, endangered species, water quality), toxic waste dumping, trespassing (timber and nontimber forest products), government services and taxes, insects and diseases, and neighbors. New insects, diseases, and wildlife (e.g., feral hogs, cogongrass, mountain pine beetle), diverse weather and climate change (e.g., hurricanes, floods, derechos, wildfires), or even poor timber market prices, forest land conversion, loss, and development make even presumably tame problems pretty wicked.

Nonprofit or NGO organizations also can experience similar problems when they manage natural resources or professional associations. They may have both land management problems and organizational problems. In fact, they must be careful to not overachieve at being a nonprofit and not even be able to break even and cover their expenses.

Finally, tameness or wickedness surely is a continuum, not a dichotomy. Problems may begin innocently and relatively simply but spin out of control as conditions and the context and the interest groups involved change. Natural resources may start with inherently wicked issues given its mix of public goods, diverse interests, local to global scales, and they are somewhat unique in this regard because of public goods, public lands, and the public interest. However, health issues such as the Covid-19 pandemic; government issues such as immigration, education, power grids, scarce budgets, and increasing public demands; and broad political issues such polarization and acrimony; all are wicked. To quote Elphaba from the play *Wicked*: "Are people born wicked, or is wickedness thrust upon them?" Natural resource and other social problems raise similar questions.

Professionalism

Professionalism is a special body of knowledge that is linked to fundamental needs and values of society. Professionalism is an enduring positive aspiration for technical disciplines that manage and protect natural resources but is more nuanced than one might think. Steinbeck (1988) stated that professionalism includes skill based on theoretical knowledge; accredited or certified education and training; membership in formal professional associations; testing of competence of individual members; adherence to an ethical code of conduct; and public service beyond simply earning a livelihood.

In a less-sanguine summary, Hill and Lorenz (2011) note positively that professionalism in real estate offers to protect society from unscrupulous, unfair, or short-term practices, through impartial advice or services. On the other hand, they note that professionalism could be criticized for circumscribing practices, controlling the knowledge base, controlling entry into the profession, demanding recognition for professional status, or fixing the market for its services. These critiques echo similar charges made by some economists and many U.S. state legislatures, who doubt the merits and costs of operating boards for licensing or registration of professions such as forestry, cosmetic arts, and general contractors and periodically call for eliminating such boards.

Discussions of professionalism are common in medical literature. Wilkinson et al. (2009) classified professionalism into themes and subthemes:

> These were organized into five clusters: (1) adherence to ethical practice principles (honesty, integrity, confidentiality, etc.); (2) effective interactions with patients and with people important to patients (courtesy, empathy, respectful, etc.); (3) effective interactions with other people working within the health system (teamwork, patience, maintain professional boundaries, etc.); (4) reliability (accountability, punctuality, organized, etc.); and (5) commitment to autonomous maintenance and continuous improvement of competence (lifelong learning, seek feedback, reflectiveness, etc.).

Even these laudable principles, however, are difficult to apply for medical professionals—for example, truthfulness about chances of dying, willingness to treat patients without proper personal protective equipment, decisions about costs of treatment versus longevity—and more (Collier 2012).

Despite the preceding qualifications, natural resource professionals—whether licensed or not—do blend skills, professional and lifelong education and training, professional associations, testing, ethics, and public service beyond simply earning a livelihood. They must maintain ethical practices; work effectively with clients and colleagues; be reliable; and pursue lifelong learning and continual improvement. Natural resource employees and managers base their professional employment on the knowledge of how to manage the earth's natural resources and activities such as soil, grasslands, forests, wildlife, fisheries, fresh and ocean water, pastures, crops, air, recreation, and other environmental goods and services.

Much of this professional knowledge has a scientific basis in biology, ecology, and ecosystems but rests just as much on anthropocentric social sciences, markets, and economic components that drive the goals and actions of natural resource management. Natural resource professionals must always blend what is possible and sustainable—biologically and ecologically—with human needs, desires, economics, and politics in order to achieve land management success, organizational profits, and community and national acceptance.

Natural resource professionals may work as employees, managers, or leaders in public or private organizations from local to international levels. We may be somewhat unique in that a large share of our jobs are in the public sector, ranging from federal land management agencies to state and local governments. As noted, many natural and wild lands are publicly owned. The resources provided by the earth are common pool (i.e., air, water, biodiversity, amenities) or collective (i.e., insect and disease, wildfire protection) goods and services that are not exclusive goods and cannot be allocated well by markets, so government involvement in allocation and management is required.

Forestry is apt to have more private sector employment for land management for real estate, timber production, or other commodities than most other natural resource careers. But even in this discipline, one-third of the U.S. forests are publicly owned. One survey estimated that there were about 40,000 forest resource professionals (Cubbage and McGinley 2020), although data for other professions were not available. Sharik et al. (2015) estimated that there were more than 12,000 natural resource university students in 2010, including about 4,000 with a natural resources major; 2,500 in forestry and in fisheries and wildlife; 1,000 in outdoor recreation; and several hundred each in range science, watershed sciences, wood sciences, and geology.

Persons in all of these disciplines may work in the private sector for business firms, developers, or environmental consulting firms; for federal, state, and local governments; for land conservancy or NGOs; or for environmental advocacy organizations. All will have professional responsibilities and need to consider the preceding dictums about professionalism in their employment.

Technocratic Traditions

There is a technocratic professional legacy for natural resource management that dates back for more than a century. Woodrow Wilson (1887) wrote a classic treatise on public administration as a new discipline to deal with complex government problems, which was the forerunner of many efforts at the turn of the century to develop professional and technical solutions to natural resource management. This essay was not famous in its day but reflected the progressive view that scientific management and administrative efficiency could improve the effectiveness of any public or private organization (Morgan et al. 2019). The progressive ideas in the 1900s were adopted by natural resource leaders from Theodore Roosevelt to Gifford

Pinchot and John Wesley Powell to Wilson again when he became President from 1912 to 1920.

Natural resource management by public agencies in the United States primarily grew out of this Progressive Era and the ideology of technocentric utilitarianism (Andrews 2006). The progressives believed natural resource managers should be value-neutral technical experts, seeking to apply the scientific method to planning and management without any political interference (Akamani et al. 2016). Data collected to inform management and planning were suspect "unless gathered by experts, analyzed by experts, and interpreted to the public by experts" (Bryan 1996; Hollinger 2020).

The evolving view of wicked problems in natural resource management reflects the demise of scientific management and Progressive Era professional autonomy as a dominant paradigm. While these paradigms were popular with experts from Theodore Roosevelt to Woodrow Wilson to Frederick Taylor as means to manage natural resources and organizations, they were largely top-down systems that subsumed the role of local communities, focusing on science and efficacy to control conflict and decide social and economic questions. This scientific approach in natural resources eventually foundered due to politics, the inability of science to decide about differences in values, and the recognition of resource management needed to consider broader adaptive governance approaches rather than narrow special interests and unilateral government decisions (Brunner and Steelman 2005).

Professionals will play various roles in their careers ranging from public or private managers to private citizens and advocates. In their employment, they should nominally be acting as neutral technical experts, carrying out the missions of their public or private organizations with skill and dedication. They should dispassionately reflect and implement the spectrum of utilitarian to biocentric orientations of their private firms to environmental nongovernment organizations (ENGOs). As leaders, they will increasingly help form as well as implement the missions and programs of their firms, agencies, and NGOs. They also may be members of and serve as leaders in professional societies that advance broad scientific and educational missions.

As citizens, professionals may pursue and advocate for different natural resource, social, recreational, religious, or political paths that reflect personal opinions, values, and passions. At times these views and organizations they join will be quite similar to their employment or at times differ from their official roles or often be completely unrelated to professional duties. As citizens and members of NGOs or professional associations, individuals also may advance throughout the ranks of membership to various levels of local and national officers. In fact, such organizations are always looking for engaged and dedicated members and officers, so advancement is even more possible than in professional positions.

In addition to professional accreditation and continuing education, professional societies offer advantages for one's career and advancement. They can help professionals build a network of colleagues for support and learn more through technical continuing education and increase personal job skills for their current job. Associations allow persons to develop contacts for getting work done on your job and meet contacts and skills to advance to another job. Associations also can help preserve networking options as life boat to escape a bad job, bad boss, bad situation, bad company, or bad luck. Associations and their meetings may give professionals more confidence, by discussing and benchmarking what others do, that they are doing the right thing on their current job, and that their organization and its foibles are no worse than many others.

Careers

Davidson (2018) described the opportunities for natural resource leadership in a career as a hierarchical progression through entry-level positions to being the enterprise executive of an organization (Figure 4.2). First, an employee or volunteer could be an individual contributor in their organization. As they demonstrate skill, talent, and accomplishments, as well interpersonal skills and smarts, they could advance to being a subject matter expert who specializes in the discipline. With more experience and success, they can rise to be a subject matter supervisor of other employees. Eventually, with continued managerial success, they could become a matrix manager, supervising many disciplines and employees; communicating laterally with other managers; and continuing to rise in their organization. Last, for the most successful, they could become the executive of an enterprise.

This process of advancement is not a linear progression necessarily, as indicated by the two- to four-way arrows in Figure 4.2. Individuals who progress usually communicate well up the chain of command as well as down and cross-train in a job or move among jobs at a similar level. "Managing upward" also is an important job skill. However, not all individuals in any direction of the management interaction are going to agree or be fair and even-handed. One must be fortunate and tactful with their supervisors, colleagues, and employees in order to succeed in all positions. Opportunities and roadblocks to success will occur in all jobs and all careers. Much advancement and job dissatisfaction does occur when supervisors or colleagues seem unreasonable, are bullies, harass workers, or are petty tyrants. Good skills and good fortune will be required to interact and move

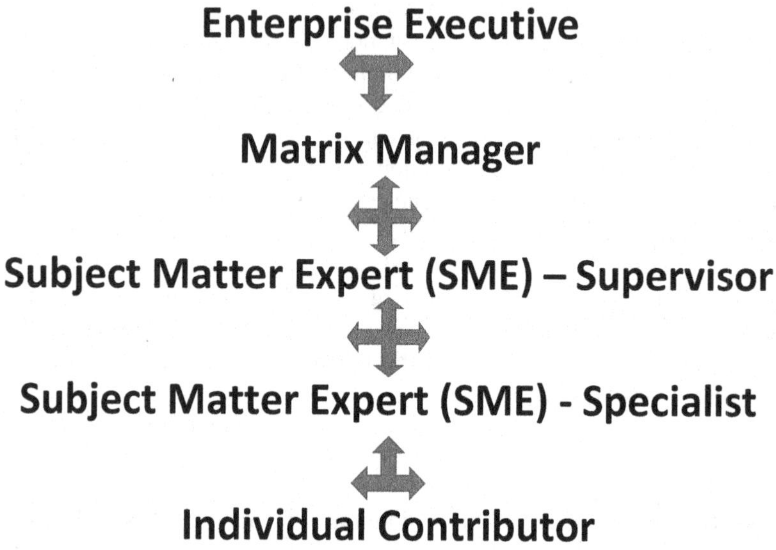

Enterprise Executive

Matrix Manager

Subject Matter Expert (SME) – Supervisor

Subject Matter Expert (SME) - Specialist

Individual Contributor

Figure 4.2 The leadership journey (Davidson 2018)
Source: Permission courtesy of Tom Davidson

successfully up, down, and laterally in the management line. If they are stuck with a hostile boss, employees may need to change employers or even careers.

Figure 4.2 does suggest that promotions in one's career can occur but infers that there are not so many levels per se that exist in any organization. Even the USDA Forest Service, for example, has only a few major professional levels: an entry-level forester to a district ranger to a supervisor, to a deputy chief to the chief. There are assistants in each of these levels, but only having four or five major levels from entry level to matrix manager and enterprise executive in any public or private organization is common. There also are technical specialists at various levels, such as for silviculture, forest management, watersheds, or wildlife. Most persons must by necessity accept and perform well at their level for most of their careers. They will not advance per se and therefore need to be satisfied with receiving "step" increases in pay and responsibility, but not major promotions.

Furthermore, many people will forgo promotions simply because they are not worth the small increase in pay or responsibility. People might prefer to live in nicer places, or close to family, or their spouses may prefer that.

Dual-career couples may trade promotions and opportunities at the expense or deferral of advancement for one person or the other. Leadership includes doing the right things for more than one's personal advancement with a balanced employment, societal, and family life.

As Morgan et al. (2019) note, one can be a leader in any job at any level and find satisfaction there as well. In fact, one probably can at least find less stress and tension at intermediate levels with less contentious human relations issues and budget authority and more enjoyable technical applications and individual project accomplishments. Leaders may excel at the positions they have, not just by climbing an organizational ladder. By being exceptionally skillful and dedicated one might be promoted, but ideally that should be a result of leadership on the job, not angling for power and importance. Also, while greater pay and plaudits may come from excellence, that is not guaranteed. Satisfaction with one's work should be sufficient and may well need to be.

A common theme in management leadership literature is that of "servant" leadership, again exemplified by Block (1996) in *Stewardship: Choosing Service over Self-Interest*. Service-oriented leaders and managers help and assist their employees, not focusing on their own power, pay, and prestige. Leaders best advance the mission and success of their organization by building leadership capacity in others. Servant leadership offers an appropriate approach for resolving broad environmental and social problems and builds on the premise that leadership paths must be open to all in order to achieve sustainability (Evans 2018).

Accordingly, with some luck and good fortune, individuals will have supportive and facilitative managers who advance the mission of their organization by providing training, mentoring, and positive formative evaluations to help employees succeed. This is not universal, of course, or maybe even common; the Dilbert cartoon strip is a sharp reflection of the foibles of management everywhere. Frustration and problems can and will occur, limiting advancement. Dead end jobs or bad managers will require luck and perspicacity to find other employment within or outside the organization.

Leadership roles and factors of success vary, but some characteristics seem common. One can be a leader in their job and organization; in their communities, professional societies, clubs, sports; or in their NGOs and nonprofits; or as activists seeking environmental or social change. The best basis for advancement in a job or a career is to be a good to great worker, hopefully with some interpersonal skills. Dysfunctional organizations or bad situations may stymie advancement and require changes in assignments, new jobs, or accepting suboptimal employment in hand for part of a career. Nonetheless, technical skills, competence, and dedication will take one far in their job and are the single best gauge of leadership potential, in the trenches or as a mid-manager. Serving effectively on project teams, committees, and broader interdisciplinary tasks can broaden one's skills and networks. This holds for both regular positions and for volunteer activities, and one can be a leader at various times in any level in an organization.

References

Akamani K, Holzmueller E., Groninger JW. 2016. Managing wicked environmental problems as complex social-ecological systems: The promise of adaptive governance. In: Melesse A, Abtew W, editors. *Landscape Dynamics, Soil and Hydrological Processes in Varied Climates*. London: Springer Geography. p. 741–762.

Andrews R. 2006. *Managing the Environment, Managing Ourselves, A History of American Environmental Policy*. New Haven (CT): Yale University Press.

Block P. 1996. *Stewardship: Choosing Service Over Self-Interest*. San Francisco (CA): Barrett-Koehler. 264 p.

Brunner RD, Steelman TA. 2005. Beyond scientific management. In: Brunner RD, Steelman TA, Coe-Juell L, Cromley CM, Edwards CM, Tucker DM, editors. *Adaptive Governance: Integrating Science, Policy, and Decision Making*. New York: Columbia University Press. p. 1–46.

Bryan H. 1996. The assessment of social impacts. In: Ewert AW, editor. *Natural Resource Management: The Human Dimension*. Boulder (CO): Westview Press. p. 145–166.

Chen JN. 2021. Sustainable investing—socially responsible investing (SRI): Environmental, Social, and Governance (ESG) Criteria. *Investopedia*. Available at: www.investopedia.com/terms/e/environmental-social-and-governance-esg-criteria.asp. Accessed 10 April 2021.

Collier R. 2012. Professionalism: What is it? *Canadian Medical Association Journal* 184(10):1129–1130.

Covey SR. 1990. *Principle-Centered Leadership*. New York: Free Press. 335 p.

Cubbage FW, McGinley KA. 2020. Sustainable forest indicator 7.50 programs, services, and other resources supporting the sustainable management of forests. 2020. In: Gen. Tech. Rep. IITF-GTR-52. Rio Piedras (PR): U.S. Department of Agriculture, Forest Service, International Institute of Tropical Forestry. p. 117–124.

Cubbage FW, O'Laughlin J, Peterson MN. 2017. *Natural Resource Policy*. Long Grove (IL): Waveland Press. 505 p.

Davidson T. 2018. From seedling to canopy: What to expect on your leadership journey. Guest Lecture, NC State University College of Natural Resources. April 5, 2018. Provided by Leadership Nature, contact at www.LeadershipNature.com.

Evans TL. 2018. Sustainable leadership: Toward restoring human and natural worlds. In: Redekop BW, Gallagher DR, Satterwaite R., editors. *Innovation in Environmental Leadership*. London: Routledge. p. 61–79.

Farley J. 2012. Ecosystem services: The economics debate. *Ecosystem Services* 1(1):40–49.

Farley J, Costanza R. 2002. Envisioning shared goals for humanity: A detailed, shared vision of a sustainable and desirable USA in 2100. *Ecological Economics* 43(2–3):245–259.

Gibran K. 1923. *The Prophet.* New York: Alfred A. Knopf, 1971 Version. 96 p.

Grint K. 2010. Wicked problems and clumsy solutions: The role of leadership. In: Brookes S, Grin S, editors. *The New Public Leadership Challenge.* London: Palgrave Macmillan. p. 169–186.

Hardin G. 1968. The tragedy of the commons. *Science* 162:1243–1248.

Hill S, Lorenz D. 2011. Rethinking professionalism: Guardianship of land and resources. *Building Research & Information* 39(3):314–319. doi:10.1080/0961 3218.2011.563051

Hollinger JC. 2020. The chiefs' challenge: Supporting a mandate for conservation planning in the national wildlife refuge system [thesis]. [Raleigh (NC)]. North Carolina State University. 142 p.

Lachapelle PR, McCool SF, Patterson ME. 2003. Barriers to effective natural resource planning in a "messy" world. *Society and Natural Resources* 16(6):473–490.

Maslow AH. 1943. A theory of human motivation. *Psychological Review* 50(July):370–396.

Millennium Ecosystem Assessment (MEA). 2005. *Ecosystems and Human Well-being: Synthesis.* Washington (DC): Island Press. 160 p.

Morgan DF, Ingle MD, Shinn CW. 2019. *New Public Leadership: Making a Difference from Where We Sit.* New York: Routledge. 425 p.

Rittel HWJ, Webber MM. 1973. Dilemmas in a general theory of planning. *Policy Sciences* 4:155–169.

Rubio M. 2020. Take economic recovery personally. *Time.* April 7–May 4, 2020. Available at: https://time.com/collection/finding-hope-coronavirus-pandemic/5820594/marco-rubio-economic-recovery-coronavirus/. Accessed 25 May 2021.

Samul J. 2020. Spiritual leadership: Meaning in the sustainable workplace. *Sustainability* 12:267. doi:10.3390/su12010267.

Sharik TL, Lilieholm RJ. Lindquist W, Richardson WW. 2015. Undergraduate enrollment in natural resource programs in the United States: Trends, drivers, and implications for the future of natural resource professions. *Journal of Forestry* 113(6):538–551.

Steinbeck K. 1988. My chance: Reflections on forestry as a profession. *Journal of Forestry* 86(3):65.

Wilkinson TJ, Wad WB, Knock LD. 2009. A blueprint to assess professionalism: Results of a systematic review. *Academic Medicine* 84(5):551–558.

Wilson W. 1887. The study of administration. *Political Science Quarterly* 11(1) (June).

5 Key Leadership Tools and Approaches in the Management Cycle

Introduction

This chapter draws on leadership principles and characteristics of natural resources to identify and discuss approaches that can be applied to natural resources leadership and management. As mentioned, there are a vast number of theories, abundant research and popular literature, as well case studies about leadership and management in general. Natural resource leadership literature is much sparser, and its context somewhat unique.

I will cover selected components of the leadership and management cycle shown in Figure 1.1 and identify useful approaches and tools that can be applied in natural resources. I will illustrate these with principles from the management and the natural resources literature, as well as my experience as a manager and a leader. My training, experience, success, and failures have been an iterative process, which have focused what components of management principles are most important, what leading authors have written that informed my views, and how these principles and applications have worked out. I will focus on several broad strategies that are crucial for several components—proficient human resource management, stating a clear vision and mission, exercising fairness and rewarding merit, and practicing openness or transparency—and then elaborate on selected specific tactics for success.

Mission and Vision

Block stressed the importance of a clear vision extolling greatness, stated simply and often, and indeed even sounding like motherhood and apple pie. He writes that "[a] vision is an expression of hope and idealism. It over-simplifies the world and implies that anything is possible" (Block 2017)

DOI: 10.4324/9781003141297-5

Contrasting a vision and mission, he states:

> A vision is really a dream created in waking hours that describes how we would like the organization to be. It differs from a mission statement, which states what business we are in and sometimes our ranking in that business. (2017, p. 105)

He notes that goals and objectives are basically predictions of what is to come. They seldom foster nearly as much employee enthusiasm and engagement as missions and visions but are the essential building blocks to achieve them. Covey (1990) lists the lack of shared vision and values, or the understanding of a vision, as the first of seven chronic problems in an organization.

Writing about military leadership, Kolenda (2001) states that vision serves as a guiding light that directs the actions of leaders, subordinates, and organizations. A vision must provide a meaningful link between these three components and inspire a spirit of devotion and duty. He continues to observe that a leader must possess the four cardinal virtues of wisdom, justice, courage, and moderation. Leaders with character and competence who are trustworthy and treat others with respect and care can inspire followers to pursue the vision. Leaders should inspire the vision as individuals by demonstrating what one ought to be. Leaders are more than mentors; they must define "why" an organization exists (Kolenda 2001). O'Farrell (2012) comments that values underpin a company's ability to achieve its objectives and must work in tandem with an organization's vision and mission statement.

Sample (2002) supports the need for leaders to have a vision with a different take in his book *The Contrarian's Guide to Leadership*. First, he opens his book stating that contrarian leaders think differently from those around them by thinking gray and free. Thinking gray means that you don't form an opinion about an important matter until you have all the facts or until circumstances force you to form an opinion and take action without recourse to all the facts. It does not mean being a skeptic or cynical, but rather seeking and accepting all information willingly and impartially and sorting it out eventually.

A leader has to imagine all the different organizational combinations in their mind and grasp how moving people around will play out and affect the bottom line. Eventually, they also must develop visions and goals that resonate with followers and discern what range of possibilities can be achieved (Sample 2002). Grand visions made top down by great leaders are not likely to succeed. Leaders must develop visions collaboratively based on the missions and context for an organization; its products and services; processes and human resources; consultation with managers and employees; assessment of markets, and evaluation of customer expectations. Gordon and Berry (2006) posit a similar role for visions—they must be achievable and practical within the current organizational and environmental context, as well as aspirational.

A broad example of a general vision for American business firms, which has several components relevant in this chapter, has been stated for years by a nonprofit organization of business CEOs called the Business Roundtable (2019). In 1997, the purpose for a corporation was stated as the "paramount duty of management and of boards of directors is to the corporation's stockholder; the interests of other stakeholders are relevant as a derivative duty to stockholders." In 2019, however, the purpose of a corporation was redefined as "[w]hile each of our individual companies serves its own corporate purpose, we share a fundamental commitment to all of our stakeholders." They provide a broad set of five values that major companies in the United States ascribe to. Relevant for this discussion, three of these include the following:

- Investing in our employees. This starts with compensating them fairly and providing important benefits. It also includes supporting them through training and education that help develop new skills for a rapidly changing world. We foster diversity and inclusion, dignity and respect.
- Supporting the communities in which we work. We respect the people in our communities and protect the environment by embracing sustainable practices across our businesses.
- Generating long-term value for shareholders, who provide the capital that allows companies to invest, grow and innovate. We are committed to transparency and effective engagement with shareholders.

Covering environmental leadership, Gordon and Berry (2006) list vision as the first of their seven most important personal leadership characteristics. They state that vision is the ability to see ahead and communicate what you see, and that creating a shared vision is the key to environmental leadership. The authors note that environmental problems are usually complex and long term, and leaders do not need overly bold visions, rather realistic ones. Environmental visions are apt to be more successful if they are striking, apt, and clear, allowing for a robust sustained pursuit of a simple vison (Gordon and Berry 2006).

Sustainability

There are many possible visions that private firms, public agencies, or NGOs may have for natural resource management, ranging from economic, social, and environmental perspectives. The three Business

Roundtable (2019) goals excerpted earlier are essentially blends of social, environmental, and economic goals, respectively, with promises of providing diversity, sustainability, and transparency in their execution. These broad goals reflect the widely accepted paradigm of sustainable development to a large extent, which can serve as useful guide for natural resource land and organizational management. One could focus on any of one of these three economic, social, and environmental legs of sustainable development as a vision for organizations in natural resources, but a brief synthesis of their merits is relevant for natural resources managers and leaders.

A century ago, in 1916, the U.S. National Park System established a mission statement that presaged our modern version of sustainable development: "to conserve the scenery of the natural and historic objects and the wildlife therein and to provide for the enjoyment of the same in such a manner and by such means as will leave them unimpaired for future generations." Drawing from the famous English conservative Edmund Burke in the late 1700s, an apropos classic statement of natural resources sustainability was made in a Washington state court decision that upheld the 1943 State Forest Practice Act and upheld without comment by the U.S. Supreme Court:

> Edmund Burke once said that a great unwritten compact exists between the dead, the living, and the unborn. We leave to the unborn a colossal financial debt, perhaps inescapable, but incurred, nonetheless, in our time and for our immediate benefit. Such an unwritten compact requires that we leave the unborn something more than debts and depleted natural resources. Surely where natural resources can be utilized and at the same time perpetuated for future generations, what has been called "constitutional morality" requires that we do.
> —State v. Dexter 32 Wash.2d 551, 70 S.Ct. 147 [1947]

These classics were forerunners of the now famous Brundtland Report of 1987 statement of sustainable development—managing for the benefits of this generation without diminishing the ability of future generations to receive similar benefits in an undiminished state (WCED 1987). Burke was perhaps the most famous conservative British statesperson of all time and clearly supported conservation in his logic, as have natural resource professionals.

One could characterize an overriding vision and goal of natural resource leadership and management as achieving that broad modern and classical paradigm of sustainable development per the Brundtland Report. This paradigm of sustainable development may have debatable points about size, scale, time period, or its merits versus exploiting natural resources to build infrastructure and human capital. Nonetheless, it still serves as a useful reference for many of our actions.

Russell Reynolds Associates (RRA 2015) describe leadership and long-term global sustainability pithily in an excellent overview. They note that we need sustainable leaders to deal with complex transnational issues, which include environmental issues of natural and food resource scarcity, our ecological footprint, and climate change. Leaders are needed to respond to social pressure to consider people, the planet, and profits and respond to the concerns of multiple stakeholders, both inside and outside the business. They state that "[s]ustainable leaders look beyond immediate, short-term gains to see the role their organization plays in the larger context."

They also observe that leaders set strategies and ensure the delivery of results that meet the triple bottom line of social, environmental, and financial performance (RRA 2015). They list a series of behaviors of sustainable leaders, including (1) promoting the company's vision, (2) operationalizing CSR, (3), obtaining top management support, (4) engaging diverse stakeholders, (5) empowering and developing stakeholders, (6) communicating with stakeholders, (7) measuring performance, and (8) setting ethical standards. In addition, they noted that a sustainability mindset was moving from "me" to "we'—a close parallel to the Level 5 Leadership found by Collins (2001) two decades before, only with "we" being the planet, not just a company. The leadership we included enlightened self-interest, long-term orientation, courage, integrity, open-mindedness, and transparency.

Sustainability is also quite flexible and can be applied to organizations as well as natural resources. Simply leaving any organization with more resources—land, labor, capital, income, or assets—reflects sustainable management and vice versa. One could term that seeking to achieve a sustainable organization, for example, one that lasts for decades. This seems like an obvious goal, but many nonprofits come and go, and even large companies and government organizations wax, wane, merge, or fail. Indeed as noted, Collins (2001) characterized the fundamental goal of the best Fifth Level leaders as being to build prosperous and enduring (sustainable) organizations.

In an empirical example natural resources study, Ma et al. (2020) analyzed the application of sustainability as a vision in the USDA Forest Service in a different context—that of how well the Forest Service has adopted broadly defined sustainability in their organization. They collected survey data from 8,875 USDA Forest Service employees about their knowledge, attitudes, opportunities, constraints, and behavior about sustainability. The employees felt that incorporating sustainability into their existing practices was better than developing new initiatives and recognized the linkages between sustainability and addressing climate change. Ma et al. (2020) concluded that success in organizational sustainability efforts required linking a shared agency vision with climate change and the management and conservation of natural resources.

Goals and Objectives

Goals and objectives are perhaps more mundane than visions and missions and less exciting as Block (2017) noted. In fact, there is less literature about objectives as well. But one must set tangible targets and measure the success in achieving them in order to succeed as a leader or an organization—to align visions and resources. Objectives can then be used by organizations to monitor, measure, and reward success for delivering products and services. This is meant to measure both the outputs of the organization and the success of the manager at achieving the goals and objectives relevant at their level of the organization.

Objectives can be used for production, services, biological and ecological targets, human resources management, stakeholder engagement and success, and almost all other components of an organization. Objectives must be specific enough to be measured, even if they are somewhat subjective. Targets such as production quantities, visitor days, cost constraints, and employee satisfaction, absence, or turnover all are metrics that can be employed to measure success and be compared with benchmarks within a firm or for a sector. In addition, such metrics can be used to monitor, measure, and reward performance by an individual, team, group, or division for an organization.

Various U.N. agreements on climate change provide an example of new definitive efforts to set visions, goals, and standards for reducing adverse effects of increasing emissions of greenhouse gases in order to provide for a sustainable planet and human welfare. The Paris Agreement of 2015 is an exceptional example of sustainable development objectives and targets in an attempt to limit the increase in global temperatures to 2 degrees Celsius above preindustrial levels. The Paris Agreement provides means for developed nations to assist developing nations in their climate change and adaptation efforts. The Agreement creates a framework for transparent monitoring, reporting, and increase in countries individual and collective climate change goals (NRDC 2021).

One popular approach for both corporate and public objective setting has been termed SMART, which stands for the following (O'Farrell 2020):

• Specific	High-level description of goal to be achieved
• Measurable	Explains how successfully achieving this goal will be measured

- Attainable   Is it possible to achieve the goal
- Relevant or realistic   Why achieving a goal matters, or realistically can be achieved
- Time frame   When can the goal be achieved by

In her book on *SMART Objective Setting for Managers*, O'Farrell (2020) explains how the method can be used not only for tangible WHAT objectives but also for behavioral HOW objectives. The approach can be applied for measuring employees' and managers' tasks; measuring business production and service tasks; measuring technical development; and assessing behavior of employees and managers. Setting SMART objectives can lay out the tasks needed to be completed, when they need to be done by, and pinpoint whether they are possible and realistic. They can be used to identify how much should be produced or how many services provided; what training or learning processes should be achieved; or how well managers succeed in meeting human resource or financial goals.

The SMART approach has been specifically used by the USDI Fish and Wildlife Service in writing National Wildlife Refuge System (NWRS) habitat and conservation management plans. For years, all NWRS management plan objectives have been required to be (1) specific (who, what, where, when, and why), (2) measurable, (3) achievable, (4) results-oriented, and (5) time-fixed (Adamchik et al. 2004). The SMART approach also has been applied by tree nurseries to assess how managers and workers meet service and production roles in their organizations.

In a summary for Fish and Wildlife Service National Wildlife Refuge System planning in the southeastern United States, Hollinger (2020) writes that SMART objectives should establish habitat condition targets and assess success in meeting them with management activities. He adds that when SMART features are absent it may be difficult to learn lessons, and planners may simply drift along without truly knowing whether they are moving in the right direction, per Meretsky and Fischman (2014). These SMART examples for objective setting are only one of many approaches, but they are indicative of the importance of setting specific measurable objectives or benchmarks that can be used to lead decisions, guide implementation, and evaluate success.

Another approach for setting objectives uses performance indicators or best policies for personnel management. Such objectives also state the key tasks that are required for individuals to perform their jobs, including production or service targets, budget and financial management, and personnel relations. A useful example of this approach is provided by Laughlin and Andringa (2007) in *Good Governance for Nonprofits*, who offer specific draft language that nonprofit boards can use for best policies for their CEOs.

Their draft verbiage suggests that CEOs must provide detailed budgets that conform with the governing board's goals and priorities, with specific summaries of planned revenues and expenses; that the CEO establish, maintain, and eliminate programs and services effectively to achieve the organization's mission and goals; that they provide effective advancement, fundraising, and public relations efforts for their organization; and that they have credible and reliable audit and compliance procedures.

Each of these broad categories then has more detailed indicators as subtasks, goals, or key performance indicators (KPIs). For example, Laughlin and Andringa (2007) suggest that budgets for nonprofits must "contain enough detail to enable accurate projection of revenues and expenses; separate capital items from operational items; monitor cash flow and subsequent audit trails; and disclose planning assumptions." They also suggest that nonprofit CEOs treat paid and volunteer staff well and do not allow conditions that are inhumane, unfair, or undignified. These examples illustrate another way one can use objectives and best policies to advance the vision and mission of a nonprofit or service organization.

Strategies, Processes, Personnel, and Performance

Recall from Figure 1.1 that there were six elements that private and public managers and leaders must consider and perform—spanning context, vision, organizational capacity, personnel, performance, and adaptive management. As noted, the leadership and management literature on all of these subjects is so voluminous that a summary of each of these in any detail is far beyond the scope of this book on natural resources leadership. I discussed the natural resources context of private and public goods in Chapter 4, summarized a broad vision of sustainability, and reviewed stating objectives earlier.

Rather than covering all the rest of the subjects in a management cycle in excruciating detail, let me focus on a few approaches and techniques that I have the most experience with and which are useful in the assessment and leadership of organizations. These strategies and tactics have helped me achieve the broad goal of sustainable development and protection of natural resources and organizations. Specifically, I will discuss human resources, fairness and merit, and openness and transparency as key approaches for successful leaders and managers.

Human Resources

Dealing with personnel, human resources, and contractors is a key component of leadership success. As noted in Chapter 1, human resources are quite possibly the most difficult part of a management and leadership job. Identifying and hiring the best persons; directing and motivating them; monitoring and rewarding performance; dealing with problems and personal issues; resolving issues of responsibility, territory, and resources; and satisfying employees or contractors are the crux of leadership and management, and they not subject to any universal rules or principles.

There are many views about best practices for personnel management, but guaranteed means to achieve success do not exist. People, individual and social values, organizational behavior and management, governments, and much more are complex, and problems and opportunities always exist. Western (2018) deftly summarizes four discourses that explain several broad paradigms of personnel management in natural resources, consisting of (1) scientific management, (2) human relations, (3) transformational leadership control, and (4) his nascent term of eco-leadership. Many initial management and leadership theories stemmed from scientific management or the Controller discourse. In business, this approach led to identification and measurement of work processes, division of labor, increasing efficiency, and assembly lines, but it was dehumanizing with employees becoming cogs in an industrial machine. This scientific management paradigm pervaded natural resource management as well in the Progressive Era and remains germane in the public and private sectors with a focus on measurement, audits, and targets to control resources to achieve efficiency. One might observe that such measurement and monitoring of jobs remain dominant in major U.S. companies such as Amazon, package delivery companies, or home health agencies, which track time, output, and even location in detail.

Western (2018) continues to note that the human relations movement, which he terms the therapist leadership discourse, presumes that happy workers are more productive workers. Leadership was desired to encourage workers to achieve their personal goals through their work, encouraging their motivation and commitment to their jobs and employers. Modern examples of worker-friendly companies seem to be Google and Facebook at least, or perhaps Silicon Valley and tech companies in general, although the amount of computer coding done per day or some other period still is commonly evaluated. Natural resource jobs surely rely on implicit emotional appeals to personal satisfaction, especially in the public sector, where public service and interactions are paramount and measurement of success elusive. It may be much easier, however, to determine how much timber is inventoried or marked in a day or whether a timber tract produces as much value when cut as when cruised. And the consequences are substantial—losing money on many tracts will cause one to lose their job.

Western (2018) progresses with the leadership discourses to describe visionary leaders who built large entrepreneurial and dynamic companies but who were still quite controlling and had conformist cultures. Individuals and teams worked because they believed in the company's vision, and those who did not were expelled. Steve Jobs at Apple and Elon Musk at Tesla certainly provide relevant examples. Western then posits a new discourse of eco-leadership composed of elements of environmental and social activism. This discourse still requires organizational and employees dialogue and a sense of community and has a more distributed sense of power among leaders, management, and workers. Such new organizations will require more harmony than conformity; more diversity in values, cultures, gender, and ethnicity; less reliance on formal organizational structures; and more reliance on spiritual beliefs, justice, and ethics.

Sample (2002) reiterates the importance of leaders in hiring, motivating, retaining, and delegating to the best persons possible, and if necessary, firing those who are counterproductive. Leaders should hire persons with skills that either complement their own shortcomings or fill an important role in the organization that will help it succeed. Sample notes that there is no such thing as the "right person for the job." The appropriate question is this the best person available for the job in the time frame that I must fill the position in? Perfection is not possible in any management action. The amount of funds available and the need to hire somebody soon often require taking the best action possible when job openings occur.

There are a variety of approaches for hiring personnel, including direct hires by persons with authority to do so, with the assistance and rules of in-house or consulting human resources if the organizations are large enough. One also can establish committees for screening applicants; use management consulting firms (headhunters); or simply develop and post position announcements and screen applicants who qualify. The government uses quite formal procedures; academic faculty use search committees; and large private industry and NGOs have formal procedures and often more pre-hire job aptitude and personal characteristics testing, but more management discretion in selecting candidates. My observation is that none of these are perfect; stellar and unwise hires occur in every sector. In my about 25 to 30 direct hires, I always tried to hire the most talented and collaborative persons that we could find and afford and attempted to keep them. With a couple of exceptions, this worked well in getting talented faculty and staff, although about a quarter of the faculty did go on to leadership positions with large salary increases either within the university or at other institutions but made great contributions to our organization while there.

Managers have many sources of power to achieve their missions and supervise employees. Classical organizational behavior literature by French and Raven identified five principal sources of management power, including legitimate, reward, coercive, expert, and referent (French and Raven 1959;

Raven 2008). Legitimate power comes from one's position in the hierarchy. Reward power includes salary, leave, promotion, job assignments. Coercive power is the negative power to punish people and best used sparingly and fairly. Expert power includes talent, knowledge, and cross-training. Referent power covers personality, charisma, networking, and charm. Positive applications of power are more apt to encourage success, but not all managers or employees may be inclined to make use of them first.

Once employees are hired, leaders should empower and delegate to them as line managers with responsibility for actually running the organization, and indeed let them make any decisions possible without interference from support staff. Staff serve important functions, but they should not exercise power of a leader while being shielded from the heat and accountability that line managers endure. Leaders also should personally perform meaningful annual reviews with employees against the goals that they each have agreed to for their job. And last, if circumstances warrant, leaders should tell failures that they would like them to leave the organization, and if they do not do so willingly, indeed they must fire them personally, which should not be delegated to subordinates (Sample 2002).

For modern complex and competitive business environments, Yuki and Lipsinger (2008) observe that flexible and resilient organizations need to be strong in the area of human capital—hiring, nurturing, and retaining skilled and talented people who are highly motivated to do their job well. Leaders can improve employee skills, motivation, and cooperation via supporting, recognizing, developing, consulting, empowering, delegating, and team building activities.

These broad discourses about leadership provide excellent principles of how leaders and managers can think of human relations but don't provide much operational guidance for natural resources. So let me focus on a couple of approaches that can be used in most organizations—fairness and transparency. These are just two of a large number of strategies and tactics that managers can use but can be crucial in achieving many desirable goals and features in management.

Fairness and Evaluations

Fairness, equity, and merit are related broad strategies to achieve management success. These precepts suggest that leaders should define and explain tasks clearly; assign them equitably among their employees and teams; and reward workers fairly based on their performance, productivity, and quality. Fairness infers that the work required in an organization is divided in proportion to the talents and pay of individuals and teams and that merit, not favoritism, is used to reward persons. Furthermore, more talented workers, managers, and leaders should contribute more. Fairness applies both to assigning jobs and responsibilities and to rewarding employees equitable for their performance. Among his numerous opportune leadership principles, Covey (1990) lists fairness as a key building block of management paradigms, followed by kindness, use and development of talent, and meaning.

Principles—In an article examining the challenges of achieving fairness, Sherf et al. (2018) describe its intentions well:

> Acting fairly is not always easy. Over 60 years of research finds that fairness is not one simple, singular choice but a complex and integrated set of decisions and actions. To be judged as fair by employees, bosses have to attend to four aspects of fairness: First, they have to ensure distributive fairness by making sure that employees are equitably rewarded for their contributions. Second, they have to follow transparent and clear procedures in arriving at those rewards. These include ensuring decisions are consistently applied across people and situations and are based on accurate information, suppressing bias in the decision process, and providing opportunities for employees to voice concerns. Third, they have to engage in informational fairness by explaining the logic behind their decisions in a timely manner. Last but not the least, they have to be interpersonally fair by treating employees with dignity and respect.

Bodanis (2020) discusses the merits of fairness as a business management strategy. He presents a number of examples where fair treatment of employees led to exceptional results. The Empire State Building was constructed in a record 13 months in 1930 to 1931, by paying workers double the going wage, paying employees even on windy days when they could not work, and giving them hot lunches. But a fair day's work was expected for the efficiency wages. Employees were still supervised closely with accountants monitoring the construction, tracking all materials, and recording attendance four times a day. Bodanis provides many other examples of where equitable treatment and respect of employees, not mean approaches, led to superior business results.

Similar to a biblical adage (Luke 12:48, which they used without attribution), Presidents Theodore Roosevelt (TR: 1908), John F. Kennedy, and George H.W. Bush all famously promoted leadership and fairness, each stating approximately: "To whom much has been given much shall be expected." This moral goal of equity of talent, reward, and responsibility has been a touchstone of American culture for centuries, as well as Western civilization.

In addition, fairness is not charity. It is more akin to merit, where employees and managers are rewarded according to their contributions—effectively meeting the organization's goals. Teachers and students, of course, do this all the time. Dedicated and talented students learn more and earn higher grades. Managers and leaders should measure, monitor, and reward performance, productivity, efficiency, and profitability. However, they must be flexible in the different types of contributions that employees can make and with variability in outputs due to customary and normal operations. New and risky ventures also require far more license than customary ones, and many operations still may have intangible outputs.

Evaluation—Fairness in management and leadership, however, can be somewhat subjective and is not easy to define and implement. Different persons have different perspectives on what is fair, and these views are colored by self-interest and different values. And almost everyone may have some ego and bias that their work is either more important than others or at least more important than recognized by management. They may believe that even if the organization agrees what is important, either the measurement of or the rewards for their relative contributions are inequitable. They also may believe that even if the measured standards for performance are made, their intangible contributions are more important than those measured. This can lead to discontent if they believe they are not being treated or rewarded fairly. Effective SMART objectives, KPIs, and other tools are crucial means to ensure fairness and transparency in measurements and rewards. Management should aim to align personal and company values in order to accomplish the organizational visons and missions (O'Farrell 2012).

In order to reward employees on merit, managers must clarify the goals and tasks to be performed, and measure performance quantitatively, and use their legitimate sources of power to skillfully encourage performance. Being fair and rewarding employees for quantified merit can help managers achieve the stated organizational mission better. But it does not necessarily lead to universal approval. Some persons who are less productive or contributing in some less measurable or subjective fashion to the mission will receive less reward and may not be satisfied. At least stating the missions and objectives and metrics clearly, and using those standards to judge performance, will help affirm organizational goals and facilitate individual success. Persons who do meet these standards better will be pleased to be rewarded for doing so and increase their efforts for the organization. Persons who are less successful may disagree, but they are more likely to accept decisions made transparently than those based on hidden agendas or favoritism. And they are more likely to change their efforts in order to achieve the stated objectives and standards.

Productivity is not absolute. As the quotes given earlier indicate, those with more talent, wealth, or social standing should contribute more. Leaders also must accommodate those with less skill or social disadvantages and help them prosper and progress. This would include special training; matching skills with job assignments; and listening and learning from staff with different gender, diversity, and life situations. Indeed, diversity in the workforce can help most organizations, because it brings different perspectives and values to the mission; helps identify weaknesses and strengths of narrow approaches; and helps broaden the appeal of goods or services to a broader customer base that reflects the diversity of the local to national population.

Limitations—Fairness also is not a guarantee of management success and may not be possible to implement even if it is desired. For example, salary compression issues in many organizations present often intractable tradeoffs between being fair to current staff members versus paying the going rate to attract new employees. Since state legislatures and even Congress do not allocate much money for raises any more, current raises have been almost nonexistent for state employees, so managers simply cannot pay them as much as new hires, who then also get locked in at their new wage rate. There is not much management discretion here, so either moves among jobs or small steps in a hierarchy or leaving for a new job is the only alternative unfortunately. Private NGOs and companies may have more flexibility to pay fair wages but presumably with less job security.

As noted, one means of identifying and measuring tasks to be performed is through establishing annual goals or KPIs for employees and managers and periodically assessing if they are met satisfactorily, or better or worse. Performance measurement can be done by production and cost data by function, activity or unit—for example, acres treated, wildlife population levels, water quality, profits—or other metrics deemed appropriate. As the product and services are delivered, employees, managers, and leaders should be rewarded roughly in proportion to their successful efforts and salary and funds available for raises, discretionary budgets possible, and personnel and program authority. However, annual evaluations can be the scourge of managers and employees. Managers surely can be autocratic, and may seek their own ratification or to favor sycophants, or ding employees for endemic or insoluble problems. Measurement, evaluation, and improvement exercises must be done with a light touch, broad understanding, and respect.

Evaluation of employees and managers can occur formally or informally. The goals, objectives, and annual evaluations mentioned before are a formal way to achieve this. Negative feedback from employees or frequent employee complaints to human resources are certainly another indicator of problems. If these occur, more formal leadership responses are needed.

Managers also can be evaluated based on their performance by methods such as "360 Reviews," which refer to evaluations by bosses, subordinates, clients, and peers. These are used frequently with some effectiveness, if the subordinates are ensured confidentiality and the peers are representative, not selected and stacked in favor of the manager or the evaluators or vice versa. These reviews also can be compared with large data banks of all other reviews of a similar nature, which provides benchmarks for the management review. The managers and the evaluators can receive scores as ordinal ranks, say 1 to 5, and a percentage rank, say 10% to 90% compared to all other evaluations done by a management consulting firm.

Managers should try to improve poor employee performance through positive encouragement, training, smaller raises, fewer promotions, or all else failing, official reprimands and penalties. They must use their sources of power and positive politics and persuasion to deal with supporters, doubters, and opponents; this is the opposite of winning through intimidation (Block 2017). Persons that continue to be unsuccessful or obstructive for extended periods should transfer to other places in the company that match their skill sets better or terminated if cause and due process occur. Conversely, if managers constantly fail at implementing their understanding of the corporate mission, perhaps it is they who should depart and find better job, value, and skills alignment within their company, agency, or elsewhere.

Note that this same broad theme of identifying goals, setting measurement metrics, evaluating success, and reforming or terminating failure could be applied to management and program evaluation. The individual metrics collected for employees should, of course, be able to be aggregated to indicate program accomplishments and effectiveness and used for benchmarks for how well managers of teams, groups, or divisions are performing, as well as broad projects and organizational units.

Openness and Transparency

As mentioned often in the preceding literature, another excellent approach for leadership and management is transparency, openness, and communication, within an organization, with external stakeholders, and with political and corporate leaders. Block (2017) mentioned this as keystone for an empowered organization. Drawing from Terry (1993), Evans (2018) notes that leaders must be concerned not only with what decisions are made, but with how they are made—decisions must be made in open and transparent ways. Leaders must treat people with respect and involve them in decisions that affect their lives and communities. Sustainable leaders acknowledge the power of average people to create meaningful and beneficial change. Leaders cannot be perfect in pursuing sustainable change but should be aware of imperfect knowledge and contradictions in facts and values yet must not be deterred by a false standard of perfection (Evans 2018).

Publicly available information facilitates meeting missions, helps understanding, and prevents gamesmanship. A cliché is that information is power. Raven (2008) later added that controlling information, which people need to accomplish something, as a "sixth" management power. Releasing information throughout an organization distributes that power, so that leaders, managers, and staff become smarter and more effective. Some modern management approaches suggest what is termed "radical transparency," sharing as much information and knowledge in the company as possible in order to build trust across all employees and teams and deliver products and services most effectively (Colvin 2015).

Transparency does build trust among leaders and employees. It brings key values, vision, issues, and data out into the open and can foster evenhanded discussion of organizational programs and success, reducing hidden agendas and political games. Transparency helps ensure that resources and actions align with missions or at least reveals what the actual priorities may be. It also is often considered as an immunization against favoritism or corruption. Managers cannot hide pet projects or dirty deals if budgets and programs are open and listed. And if managers cannot defend what is presented, the allocations are probably not fair or wise. With full information on programs, productivity, and costs, leaders and employees can more deliberately discuss the merits of different approaches and funding in order to meet the stated missions and objectives and be more confident that the best programs receive priority.

Transparency and openness in making decisions also can be institutionalized by open decision-making with the public and stakeholders. The Programme for Endorsement of Forest Certification (PEFC 2017) provides an excellent set of requirements for setting forest certification standards every 5 years by their member country certification systems. A detailed 18-page document sets forth transparent standard setting procedures, which require that each PEFC country certification system

- identify and map all specific stakeholders,
- make public announcements of the process,
- establish a balanced working group of these stakeholders,
- consult the public,
- perform pilot tests of the revised standards, and
- approve and publish the standards.

The Center for Food Integrity (2017) developed a seven-step circular Transparency Model that summarizes key points for organizations communicating with the public, which are applicable within an organization as well. First, organizations should share their *motivations* and act in an ethical manner, consistent with stakeholder interests. Second, *disclosure* requires them to share all information, both positive and negative. Third, *stakeholder participation* requires firms to engage those interested in the business. Fourth, firms should share information stakeholders deem *relevant*. Fifth, *clarity* mandates that firms share information that is easily understood and obtained. Sixth, *credibility* indicates that firms should share positive and negative information and operate with integrity. Last, *accuracy* states that organizations should be truthful, objective, reliable, and complete. This list summarizes the tenets of internal transparency as well and is a useful benchmark for leaders and managers.

The Economist (2021) provides an interesting take on personality types that meshes with the nexus between openness and human resources. In business, about 40% of the population or workers are extroverts, 40% are introverts, and 20% are ambiverts who display both characteristics. This matters for how managers should approach information flow, meetings, and consultation. Better preparation and openness will ensure that extroverts, who tend to prefer and dominate ad hoc discussions, do not influence decisions too much. More preparation and distribution of materials in advance will help introverts prepare and reflect and have equal opportunity (Economist 2021). As natural resource professionals who want to work outside, we are probably closer to at least 75% introverts, so managers and leaders must consciously strive to encourage discussion from recalcitrant employees. Managers also should be at somewhat reserved in their communication approaches, and not overly promotional, or they will turn quiet people off.

For example, I have learned that in traditional in-person meetings of up to a dozen or more persons regarding important or contentious issues, one can ensure that all views are heard and better discussion occurs if the leader or a committee chair presents a straightforward summary of an issue, notes that there may be lots of ways to resolve it, and then simply goes around the table and asks each person for their opinion. Many employees, stakeholders, and peers do hold back in private and public meetings for fear of being unpopular or of retribution, but simply asking everybody what they think helps a lot in generating productive viewpoints, ideas, and discussions.

A critical role of any leader is assigning best persons to lead and contribute to a team or committee, which are crucial in analyzing problems and assessing opportunities and achieving organizational missions. Small units of a few persons can interact well, and insights and dedication matter much more than flamboyance and talk. One should appoint team and committee members and tasks according to their skills and their commitment to the mission. This helps in developing and vetting proposals for broad discussion and implementation. Team leaders provide feedback up to line managers; committee members bring recommendations for new action (or inaction) to the full management team or governing board. In many organizations, all major policy actions must be referred to and reported out of a committee, just like Congress, before they will be considered by the management team, reducing wasted time. This advances best policies and promotes full discussion.

For management and governing boards, setting a well-structured agenda with specific time allocations and Robert's Rules of Order with a light touch also is surprisingly effective at ensuring that key organizational items are discussed even-handedly. The rules require clearly worded committee motions brought to a board, or an individual may make a motion, which must require a second. Then deliberate discussion is specifically required before votes are taken for or against a motion. This encourages open and transparent progress, while reducing gaming by managers, or wasting time on individual pet projects, which may not even get a second, or surely not many votes if not significant or prepared well. Then any decisions made must be implemented by line managers, employees, or staff as appropriate.

If quantitative measures of program costs and benefits and success are developed and displayed, better decisions and understanding about resource allocation will occur. Openness also helps individuals and teams feel that their opinions have been heard and consulted and understand why the selected paths have been chosen. Managers still will have to make hard decisions about competing interests and scarce resources, but employees will be far more willing to defer and accept these calls when decisions are transparent and made with some due process.

Overall, transparency and openness provide excellent foundations for decision-making processes and confidence in outcomes based on fair and objective measures, for individuals within an organization; for stakeholders; for customers and the public who purchase products or services; and for investors or policy makers who provide funding and support for organizations.

References

Adamchik RS, Bellantoni ES, DeLong Jr. DC, Schomaker JH, Hamilton DB, Laubhan MK, Schroeder RL. 2020. *Writing Refuge Management Goals and Objectives: A Handbook*. U.S. Department of the Interior, U.S. Fish & Wildlife Service, National Wildlife Refuge System, 2004. 30 p. Available at: www.fws.gov/refuges/policiesandbudget/pdfs/WritingRefugeGoals_022504.pdf. Accessed 14 March 2020

Block P. 2017. *The Empowered Manager, Second Edition: Positive Political Skills at Work*. Hoboken (NJ): Wiley. 213 p.

Bodanis D. 2020. *The Art of Fairness: The Power of Decency in a World Turned Mean*. London (UK): Little Brown Book Group. 336 p.

Business Roundtable. 2019. Corporate governance: Business roundtable redefines the purpose of a corporation to promote "an economy that serves all Americans." Available at: www.businessroundtable.org/business-roundtable-redefines-the-purpose-of-a-corporation-to-promote-an-economy-that-serves-all-americans. Accessed 13 April 2021.

Center for Food Integrity. 2017. Transparency model. Available at: www.food-integrity.org/about/who-we-are/trust-building-transparency/. Accessed 27 February 2017.

Collins J. 2001. Level 5 leadership—The triumph of humility and fierce resolve. In: *On Leadership*. Boston (MA): Harvard Business Review Press, 2011. Reprint R0507M. p. 115–136.

Colvin G. 2015. The benefit of baring It all: The 21st century corporation: Transparency. Fortune 10 December 2015. Available at: https://fortune.com/2015/12/10/workplace-transparency-benefits/. Accessed 12 February 2020.

Covey SR. 1990. *Principle-Centered Leadership*. New York: Free Press. 335 p.

Evans TL. 2018. Sustainable leadership: Toward restoring human and natural worlds. In: Redekop BW, Gallagher DR, Satterwaite R, editors. *Innovation in Environmental Leadership-Introduction*. London: Routledge. p. 61–79.

French J, Raven B. 1959. The bases of social power. In: Cartwright D, editor. *Studies in Social Power* Ann Arbor (MI): Institute for Social Research p. 150–167.

Gordon JC, Berry JK. 2006. *Environmental Leadership Equals Essential Leadership: Redefining Who Leads and How*. New Haven (CT): Yale University Press. 164 p.

Hollinger JC. 2020. The chiefs' challenge: Supporting a mandate for conservation planning in the national wildlife refuge system [thesis]. [Raleigh (NC)]. North Carolina State University. 142 p

Kolenda C. 2001. What is leadership? Some classical ideas. In: Kolenda C, editor. *Leadership: The Warrior's Art*. Carlisle (PA): Army War College Foundation Press. p. 3–25.

Laughlin FL, Andringa RC. 2007. *Good Governance for Nonprofits*. New York: American Management Association. 210 p.

Ma Z, Steele D, Cutler A, Newcomb K. 2020. Promoting sustainability in public natural-resource agencies: Insights from the USDA Forest Service. *Journal of Forestry* 118(2):105–123.

Meretsky VJ, Fischman RL. 2014. Learning from conservation planning for the U.S. National Wildlife Refuges. *Conservation Biology* 28(5):1415–1427.

NRDC. 2021. Paris agreement summary. Available at: www.nrdc.org/stories/paris-climate-agreement-everything-you-need-know#sec-summary. Accessed 21 May 2021.

O'Farrell I. 2012. *Values-Not Just for the Office Wall Plaque*. Dublin, Ireland: Evolution Consulting. 187 p.

O'Farrell I. 2020. *SMART Objective Setting for managers: A Roadmap*. Dublin, Ireland: Evolution Consulting.

PEFC. 2017. Standard-setting—Requirements. Programme for Endorsement of Forest Certification. Available at: www.pefc.org/standards-implementation/adapting-global-standards/developing-national-standards. Accessed 21 May 2021.

Raven B. 2008. The bases of power and the power/interaction model of interpersonal influence. *Analyses of Social Issues and Public Policy* 8(1):1–22. December.

Rubio M. 2020. Take economic recovery personally. *Time*. April 16, 2020. Available at: https://time.com/collection/finding-hope-coronavirus-pandemic/5820594/ marco-rubio-economic-recovery-coronavirus/. Accessed 21 May 2021.

Russell Reynolds Associates (RRA). 2015. Sustainable leadership: Talent requirement for sustainable enterprises. Available at: www.russellreynolds.com/en/ Insights/thought-leadership/Documents/RRA%20-%20Accelerating%20Sustainable%20Business%20Leadership.pdf. Accessed 15 April 2021.

Sample SB. 2002. *The Contrarian's Guide to Leadership*. San Francisco (CA): Jossey-Bass. 197 p.

Sherf EN, Gajendran RS, Venkataramani V. 2018. Research: When managers are overworked, they treat employees less fairly. *Harvard Business Review*. Available at: https://hbr.org/2018/06/research-when-managers-are-overworked-they-treat-employees-less-fairly. Accessed 14 February 2020.

State v. Dexter 32 Wash.2d 551, 70 S.Ct. 147 [1947].

Terry RW. 1993. *Authentic Leadership: Courage in Action*. San Francisco (CA): Josey-Bass Publishers. 315 p.

The Economist. 2021. Bartleby: Winning personality. 438(9237):59.

Western S. 2018. The eco-leadership paradox. In: Redekop B, Gallagher DR, Satterwhite R, editors. *Innovation in Environmental Leadership*. New York: Routledge. p. 48–60.

World Commission on Environment and Development (WCED). 1987. *Our Common Future*. United Nations World Commission on Environment and Development. Oxford (UK): Oxford University Press. 383 p. [Brundtland Report].

Yuki G, Lipsinger R. 2008. Capital ideas: Enhancing the power of human assets. *Leadership in Action* 28(2):3–24.

6 Two Leadership Cases from Government and Nongovernment Organizations

Cases and Principles

In my career as a professional, I have served as an employee, manager, and leader in state and federal research, education, and management organizations, as well as a blue-collar worker in my youth. I also have been a volunteer and an elected officer in several professional associations. A large share of natural resource professionals work for federal, state, or local government, which have similar characteristics as government bureaucracies of some type, including public budgeting, government career paths, personnel and land management responsibilities, and both substantial opportunities and constraints on their management and careers. Professional employment in the nonprofit sector or NGOs has increased considerably for natural resource professionals as well, including in professional and trade associations, NGO and environmental (ENGO) citizen interest groups, and land conservancies.

Government organizations generally have extensive hierarchical structures, formal procedures and rules, and limited management flexibility. Small nonprofits have more flexible governance with mixed board and staff division of power and authority. One can be a worker and a leader at any level of an organization, but there is more official authority and responsibility at higher-level positions with increasing personnel and budget responsibilities. My experience as a low- to middle-level manager in several government organizations and NGOs provides useful examples of leadership that natural resource professionals may encounter in their careers.

The preceding principles and discussion in this book frame a relatively unified theory of leadership—aligning resources and actions with one's stated intentions—and provide a few broad strategies to accomplish that goal. However, the discussion still could use tactics and tangible examples to illustrate the principles. While venerable, the international and national

DOI: 10.4324/9781003141297-6

individuals discussed previously are somewhat distant from what most natural resource professionals will experience in their careers.

My management and leadership efforts were motivated by the broad vision of sustainability—managing and protecting the earth's land and my organization's resources for the present and for the future. This required leadership in accomplishing the organizations' missions, while improving the employment climate, personnel skills, and finances of the organization in the future. In each case, I consciously drew on sustainability concepts for the organization and identified the specific missions and visions. While they all had similar visions of sustainable development, each situation had diverse missions, so choosing what objectives were most important and which ones to focus on was crucial.

After selecting or reaffirming visons and objectives, the strategies and tactics that I used depended on the context and the application to each job or issue. In each of these cases, I also followed the key steps in the managerial and leadership cycle shown in Figure 1.1 in Chapter 1. These included scoping the context of the organization and issues; determining our goals and objectives; choosing strategies and tactics to achieve those goals; trying to measure and assess success; and adapting approaches based on operational success or failure.

As noted in the preface, I had a moderate amount of line management experience and training in my career; was an avid reader of books on organizational management and natural resource leaders, and of articles in *Fortune* and *The Economist*; was a policy science researcher; and had innumerable discussions with and observations of other managers. Based on those foundational sources and my employment experience, my evolving goals and tactics as a leader and a manager could be listed as follows:

- Identify and focus on the real mission
- Reward merit that meets that mission, not politics
- Be open, authentic, and transparent
- Be inclusive—seek input from employees, members, clients, customers
- Listen, respond, and use that input as appropriate
- Base analyses on the best data available
- Be perceptive/realistic/skeptical of grand plans and promises
- Be collaborative
- Analyze alternatives and act
- Be honest/candid/respectful/courteous
- Be humorous and humble
- Lead by example—perform the jobs that I asked of others

Most of the preceding tenets are self-explanatory, but four principles of vision, competent personnel management, fairness, and transparency do run throughout them. I always tried to identify and stress the importance of the core missions of the organizations I worked for and to share the data, budgets, work, planning, and implementation of our responsibilities. In planning and as an operational manager, I sought input from the employees and used that to set objectives and tactical plans for the teams I directed—a USDA Forest Service Southern Station Research Work Unit (1991–1994) and the NC State University Department of Forestry (1994–2004).

Science and Education Administration

The first case of applying leadership and management principles in my career covers my experience as a primary-level manager and leader in two organizations—a Project Leader for the USDA Forest Service Southern Research Station Branch and a Head of the Department of Forestry (and eventually) Environmental Resources at NCSU. These two organizations are representative of federal government and academic institutions in the United States and operate somewhat similarly to other state and local government organizations. I also worked as a recreation aide for the Forest Service in California one summer and as state Service Forester in Kentucky for 2 years. National Forest land management organizational procedures were not much different than research, and state universities and state agencies share much in common.

The USDA Forest Service has about 30,000 permanent and 15,000 seasonal employees and is probably the largest federal natural resources employer (Cubbage et al. 2020). It manages about 193 million acres of federal land, second only to the US Department of Interior (USDI) Bureau of Land Management, which has 248 million acres. The next two largest land managers in the United States are USDI Fish and Wildlife Service with 89 million acres, and the National Park Service with 80 million acres (Gorte et al. 2012). NC State is a public Land Grant University with about 35,000 students and 9,000 faculty and staff. Its missions are education, research, and extension, similar to Land Grants in most of the U.S. states, as well as many other universities.

The key organizational missions for research, education, and extension might be briefly stated as delivering high-quality service outputs given the personnel, funding, infrastructure, and other inputs available. Our goals were generally producing quality science and education products and graduates who would contribute to all levels of natural resource professions, from practitioners in the woods, fields, rivers, and swamps to leaders in business sectors and state and local governments. Our strategies and tactics usually involved field research and instruction for the biological and social sciences, as well as analytical, statistical, geographic information systems (GIS) training, economic, and policy skills. We measured success based on students graduated, grants received, publications, and extension activities and contacts made. Based on informal and formal assessments, at the individual level and departmental level, we rewarded people when possible with the moderate federal or meager state increases in budgets.

Organizational Context

Research and education are service professions, and key objectives include providing quality instruction, innovation, and outreach to students, practitioners, and citizens. The details of vision, strategy, tactics, performance measurement, outcomes assessment, and continual improvements apply for public organizations. The key organizational context was that they were public agencies with considerable institutional history; extensive policies, procedures, and regulations; and formal hierarchical management structures. Employees were civil service employees, professors, and staff, who were usually dedicated, and relatively independent as scientists, and had considerable job security. Both federal and state organizations mandated that unit managers must balance their annual operating budgets. The key missions and visions of these institutions were not new—excellence in research, plus teaching and extension—but they still did need to be discussed and reaffirmed to be sure everyone understood and agreed.

To focus on our vision at the USDA Forest Service, the first effort I pursued was to write my views in a draft strategic plan for our economics research work unit and then seek input from the scientists in the unit through several meetings and revisions, and then we jointly developed objectives and implementation procedures in the scientists' job descriptions. In the plans, we reaffirmed our long-standing commitment to core forest economics, markets, and policy research, and added nontimber valuation as an explicit mission. We had recently been merged with an economics of forest protection (insects, disease, fire) unit, and we also actively affirmed that we would excel in that area. So we focused considerable research efforts in that subject in cooperation with Washington Office staff in order to solidify that discipline and our research funding in that subject area. We did not plan it explicitly but soon seized a rare international Forest Service grant opportunity to obtain an international project in southern Brazil based on prior research as well. All of these timber market, forest protection, and international research areas prospered for the next three decades under subsequent leaders and scientists.

At NC State, I sought to make sure we followed our three core missions—teaching, research, and extension—and measured accomplishments. This required treating all persons in the three core roles fairly. I focused on praising and rewarding teachers of undergraduate classes or advisors of graduate students the most, who were less recognized and paid much less than faculty members who had mostly research appointments when I arrived. Similar to almost all Research I universities, researchers received more benefits from pay to operating budgets and labs. I tried to redress this by stressing that teaching was our first mission, seeking to have everyone teach something, doing so myself, and stressing the equal importance of all faculty careers to our core missions. This linkage of core missions to rewards extended to extension as well, although the metrics for success focused on outreach via workshops or extension publications and some academic journals.

The tools and power that a line manager has in a scientific and educational organization are more substantial than often believed. Tenure track professors have or are seeking tenure (although they now are becoming much scarcer than non-tenured positions), and federal scientists are civil service employees. However, in both cases, scientists and professors must prepare job descriptions or statements of work, have annual evaluations, be subject to reviews, and (with a lot of effort) be subject to dismissal for failure to perform their job. More relevant operational science organization management powers are the ability to assign raises, assign administrative or task force work, allocate budgets by person or program, make teaching assignments, allocate space, facilitate or thwart grant applications, and make committee assignments. In reality, these powers are so important that very few science employees are willing to speak out much against management. In fact, leaders must actively encourage open discussion and opinions by surprisingly timid employees.

Surely given the considerable power managers have even in the public sector, they must be even more formidable in the private sector. Indeed my colleagues there have observed that considerable alignment in organizational values, solid performance, and limited candor are generally wise. The management powers in an activist group clearly are less substantial, since all the participants are volunteers. So it takes more agreement in values, networking, charm, and good reasoning to be an effective leader in these organizations. However, employment in an NGO, ENGO, or land conservancy can probably range from quite structured to more flexible depending on the director and culture.

Vision and Planning

As noted, as a line manager with the Forest Service and NC State University, I initiated organizational efforts within a few months of my appointment to prepare a clear, inclusive, comprehensive strategic plan linked to the existing organizational missions of federal forest resources research and state land grant education, respectively. The objective of these efforts was to seek and summarize important and key missions of the research work unit and academic department and to actively engage all the employees in the discussion. I tried to foster discussion, while being reserved and deferring to employees in these planning efforts. However, I did actively lead plan implementation as a manager. At times, this process could trouble current vested research interests, particularly as we broadened our programs from predominantly timber management and wildlife to more conservation biology, natural resources, and environmental technology.

In both organizational planning and management operations, to mollify hard feelings or fears or defray tensions, I tried to be humorous at the appropriate moments. Gordon and Berry (2006) note that the use of humor can be important to illustrate and resolve differences, if used naturally and without malice. They wrote that self-deprecating humor from a leader can help others talk freely, although one should not pretend to be a stage comic. Obviously, as noted earlier, Ding Darling made a career as a humorist and a conservationist. Xu (2020) reviews the use of humor in business, including (1) self-enhancing humor to encourage oneself; (2) affiliative humor to encourage social warmth and relationships; (3) aggressive humor, which generates adverse results; and (4) self-deprecating humor, which may have merit in moderation. The review found that positive uses of humor generally encouraged organizational success and helped leadership styles, but critical humor had negative impacts (Xu 2020).

Transparency

As a manager, I was as transparent as possible and related the accomplishments that we measured to the services we were producing. This helped align our resources and actions with our stated intentions. This stemmed from my reading the first book by Block (1987) in a leadership training course almost as soon as I started with the Forest Service. We identified our missions, visons, and objectives in the strategic planning, and I measured and monitored it with annual summaries and reports for the Research Work Unit and for the Department of Forestry.

This transparency included preparation and distribution of all our budget income and expenses by program line area each year, as well as full summaries and spreadsheets of all our research publications grants, courses taught, and extension products. This approach of publishing transparently all income and expenses—from the Washington Office allocation by major research line to the Southern Research Station to the Research Work Unit, with cuts for administration and physical lab maintenance and operating—was used by my two station directors at the Forest Service Southern Research Station, which I adopted as well. It worked well there, as it did when I used that approach at NC State.

At both the Forest Service, and at NC State, I summarized all the sources of funds from our organizational or grant budgets and the amount that each program and rank of persons received. I did not release individual salaries, but curious staff could look up state salaries if they wanted to. At the Forest Service, I gave more funds to PhD scientists for operating and for cooperative research contracts, and smaller amounts of operating funds for MS scientists, and listed that. This transparent difference did create some dissatisfaction but at least fostered useful discussions about technical merit and ability to lead versus support research efforts.

At NC State University, I listed academic, research extension, federal McIntire-Stennis formula funds, development or forest management proceeds, grants, etc., and all the allocations to major budget line items such as academic salaries, research salaries, staff salaries, individual programs (biotechnology, research co-ops, woodlot forestry, Christmas trees). I also listed allocations of the modest amount of funds for faculty to spend per year by professorial rank, with more for young faculty, and the amount that I allocated for my administration and travel. Any special projects that I budgeted for also were listed. I gave the full details to all my faculty as a hard copy and discussed it with my Deans.

Table 6.1 shows an example of our old FY 2003 North Carolina State Forestry Department annual budget that I distributed. Note that the total discretionary operating funds of about $1 million were respectable for an academic unit, although they seemed scarce and were cut every year, eventually wiping out much of those funds in the 10 years that I was Head. With the funds available, I was able to focus on key programs such as graduate research assistantships and still distribute some funds to every program and every faculty member in the department. The table shows that I was able to allocate about $85,000 in support for individual faculty and $135,000 to our major research programs, as well as $285,000 in graduate student stipends, which was pretty much at that time. Current austere academic times have seen such funds dwindle greatly, so harder allocation decisions must be made, and fewer friends can be acquired by budgeting.

At NC State, I also prepared an annual summary report of all major courses taught, publications, grants, and extension workshops. I prepared and distributed anonymous individual accomplishment worksheet summaries of these data, which were then used as the key basis for discussing responsibilities and assigning raises. As noted, the university nominally espoused teaching and undergraduates as their primary mission, but teachers

Table 6.1 Simplified NCSU Department of Forestry Operating Budget Information, FY 2003 ($)

Fund source/ Budget item	Academic	ARS Research	ARS-Xmas	Mc-Stennis	Overhead	Foundation	Total
Income	1753963	903678	225138	356375	143522	258000	4006174
Base budget income with salaries							
operating budget expenses—allocations							
Grad Student salary	65000	55000		95000	0	0	285000
Personnel/obligated exp.(-)							
Added FY03 OpExp	10000	10000					20000
Courses/teaching	12000						12000
Greenhouse rent		5000					5000
Allocations							
TIP Salary		20000					20000
Undergrad/grad Directors	5000						10000
Asst Profs 5.25@5K		16000	5000				31000
Assocs Prof 5@4K		16000					20000
Full Profs 7.25@3K		18000					23000
GIS Salary	20000						20000
Overhead Rebates							
Subtotal	25000	70000	5000	0	42000	0	166000
Miscellaneous							
Subtotal	0	21000	0	0	21000	20000	72000

(Continued)

Table 6.1 (Continued)

Fund source/Budget item	Academic	ARS Research	ARS-Xmas	Mc-Stennis	Overhead	Foundation	Total
			Base budget income with salaries				
Income	1753963	903678	225138	356375	143522	258000	4006174
			operating budget expenses—allocations				
Co-op/research/extension Programs (approx.)							
Biotech – Release							130000
CAMCORE		13000		20000		7000	80000
Hardwood				10000			87000
Nutrition	20000						20000
Rooted Cutting				10000			30413
Tree Improvement				10000			43785
Woodlot – Release	20000						20000
Wildlife	10000					10000	20000
GIS				10000			10000
Economics						10000	100638
FEOP	5000						49582
Extension							13582
Subtotal	55000	13000		60000		27000	605000
Total Allocations	**167000**	**174000**	**5000**	**155000**	**63000**	**47000**	**1165000**

FWC 12 January 2003; Version #1; zip#3\soperatingbudget.FY2003.12jan2003; reduced form

Note 1: Columns do not sum to totals in this example because some programs not included.

Note 2: Does not include separate departmental "pass through" budgets for Extension ($800,000); State research ($181,000); Research co-ops ($1,726,000), New external grants ($4,264,367), for a total of $6,971,367

seldom have the best salaries, resources, or rewards. To focus on the stated mission, based on tallies of courses and credit hours, I assigned the highest raises closely in proportion to those who taught the most or advised the most graduate students. Researchers also could contribute a lot by teaching undergraduate classes and advising many graduate students, and I rewarded the few who did so equally well. My administrators seemed a little ambivalent about rewarding teachers more than big grant winners but could hardly contest my focus on the university's widely promoted key mission. With extensive faculty dialogue, I also established productivity benchmarks for teaching, research, and extension, which were useful for annual evaluation and promotion discussions.

I was fortunate to serve as Department Head in the decade from 1994 to 2004; while it seemed tough at the time and that funds for salary increases were never enough, they at least were 3% to 5% per year. The decade of the 2010s has seen the North Carolina state legislature reduce funding for raises drastically, probably averaging less than 2% per year at best. This impoverishment of public employees makes exhortation, charm, flexible work, and operating support the key positive tools to encourage performance in achieving our academic and agency organizational missions, unfortunately. And the pervasive fear of not getting tenure or a poor post tenure review still motivates faculty regardless of no raises.

Practice and Priorities

I made specific efforts to practice what I was leading, by publishing papers as a scientist, teaching or helping with a course or two per year as Department Head, advising graduate students, getting grants, and talking at extension meetings. This principle follows a widely quoted adage attributed to Stephen Covey (1990), which stated that "[w]hat you do has far greater impact than what you say." Leading in this fashion contributes to the mission of the organization, helps demonstrate that the work is not so challenging as to be unsurmountable, and helps remind leaders how difficult practicing the mission can be, so they do not make unrealistic exhortations for the troops to work harder. As Head, I also tried to keep an open door policy whenever I was in, and kept my boots and travel bags ready to visit with professors, projects, students, classes, and stakeholders in the field, which we all enjoy in natural resources.

Of course, almost every person believes that their work is uniquely important and more deserving of individual raises or program funding, but having transparent good data and simple discussions prevent most pettifoggery. It also helps to encourage persons to contribute more based on the data demonstrating their relative accomplishments. Similarly, many scientists want to build their program and empire, seeking hard money salary support from the state, not soft money from their own grants. I supported some but not all of these requests, again focused on simple metrics—graduate student support and advising, teaching undergraduates, grants, and publications— thereby supporting true stars who return more than the moderate academic funds one can spare among many competing interests.

However, nascent stars do need to support the core missions, not just the promise of productivity. They might be convincing in getting new funds in the short run based on early accomplishments and charm but need to become more productive and more self-supporting with time. This same practice would not be hard to implement for almost all natural resource disciplines—based on area managed, timber harvests area and volume planned and made, reforestation area, restoration area, prescribed fires, wildlife diversity, water quality, public meetings, plans approved, etc.

My two experiences as a line manager, with about 8 and 60 or more direct reports and a $1 million to $10 million budget, respectively, were challenging. Despite focusing on and rewarding fairly accepted missions of research, teaching, and extension, not everyone was thrilled all the time. Many believed that their program or efforts deserved more support; persons who wanted to manipulate outcomes preferred less transparency. However, the transparency approach of publishing all income and expenditures and outputs prevented most squabbles, as long as the rewards roughly aligned with numerical accomplishments.

A famous perspective by TR—The Person in the Arena—does describe the hazards of politics and leadership. Note that the inference here is that of a gladiator in the sand (arena) of the Roman Coliseum. The speech is still referred to often today and bears quoting to conclude this section on how managers at all levels might feel—as well as politicians (Roosevelt 1910):

> It is not the critic who counts; not the man who points out how the strong man stumbles, or where the doer of deeds could have done them better. The credit belongs to the man who is actually in the arena, whose face is marred by dust and sweat and blood; who strives valiantly; who errs, who comes short again and again, because there is no effort without error and shortcoming; but who does actually strive to do the deeds; who knows great enthusiasms, the great devotions; who spends himself in a worthy cause; who at the best knows in the end the triumph of high achievement, and who at the worst, if he fails, at least fails while daring greatly, so that his place shall never be with those cold and timid souls who neither know victory nor defeat.

Leadership and Governance for Nonprofits

There are thousands of nonprofits and nongovernmental organizations in the United States and the world, which may be categorized as professional associations, trade associations, or citizen interest groups. The management cycle and organizational context for a nonprofit are different than that of a public or private organization. In our disciplines, professional associations such as the Wildlife Society (TWS), SAF, or the Range Society help set professional standards; disseminate science to members and the public through publications, meetings, and professional certification; promote their professions; and advocate science-based policies for management, conservation, and protection of their particular natural resource. A trade association, such as the American Forest and Paper Association or Electric Power Research Institute, represents the business, political, or even scientific interests of a given sector of the manufacturing or service economy. Citizen interest groups such as the Sierra Club, Audubon Society, or Greenpeace provide information and education, perform lobbying or direct action advocacy and protests, pursue legal strategies, and seek international policies to promote conservation of their principal conservation or environmental interests (Cubbage et al. 2017).

The goals of nonprofits and NGOs are to achieve their missions as paraphrased earlier, with the budgets that they are able to generate from member dues, meetings, publications, grants, or other sources. Success at promoting the profession, managing a public good, or protecting a natural resource is hard to measure, although every sector does monitor and participate in various educational, policy, and advocacy efforts and tries to claim significant credit for any issues that they are involved in relating to their members. Summaries of policies affected, bills passed, federal or state regulatory rules changed or prevented, and other policy outputs are one way to measure success. So are publications, magazines, newsletters, annual budgets, financial statements, and membership numbers. Success of their staff is linked to these outcomes. Increasing (or decreasing) budgets and paying members and dues are continual issues, and a variety of approaches are tried to solve these core problems.

Organizational Context and Vision

The **organizational context** for a small nonprofit or NGO is much different from government and university management. The federal government and state universities have major institutional support and detailed regulations and thousands of employees in each organization, and it is very difficult to make written policy changes at any level and almost impossible for low- to middle-level managers. Nonprofits such SAF, TWS, or the Fisheries Society are far different. There are only a modest number of staff—10 to 30—and few rules and regulations per se. While it seems excruciating during the process of debate in a large governing board of an NGO, they can make moderate or even major changes in their plans and operating policies relatively quickly.

The typically small organizations and staff size also makes the governance and employment situation much different, magnifying both the positive and negative personal interactions; human resource issues; (lack of) chain of command; budget swings; and board, staff, and member interactions. Essentially, a governing board sets and makes nonprofit or NGO policies and monitors performance; a director or CEO helps set policies, executes the policies and practices, and directs the staff; and technical staff deliver the programs. As a professional, you may be involved in any one of the three parts of this triangle, which usually work well but require some negotiation at times.

Professional associations, citizen interest groups, homeowners associations, sports leagues, and a host of others have boards, who are elected or appointed by the current board or staff. They may have representatives based on geographical area or on a technical specialty. These boards usually are a form of representative democracy with each board member representing his or her region and the broad interests of the association to make policies about actions, programs, and budgets. Governing boards generally are effective means to set NGO policies and channel member opinions to the professional executives and staff but are not without hazards such as little diversity, indecision, inattention, or court packing. In addition, having large boards often does make for extended discussion and debate about policies, and a majority of the board must vote to change any policy or rule.

In each of my 3-year terms as a SAF board member (termed "the Council" in my first stint), we developed a number of strategic plans and discussed three or four management books. One of these in particular provides a stellar example of how aligning intentions with actions matters and the opportunity and challenges of doing so. In my second term at SAF, I was elected as Vice-President, which involved a year in that role, a year as President, and a year as Past President. Our new governing document during that period was a Board Policies Manual (BPM), initiated and approved the year before I began my term on the Board. That manual was drawn quite closely from a concise guide and book by Laughlin and Andringa (2007), which included specific language for policies that all organizations could consider for good governance.

Laughlin and Andringa (2007) state that good policies determine actions and success of nonprofit organizations. They divided their description of such policies into sections on organization essentials; vision, mission, short-term goals; governing board structure and processes; members, officers, committees, finances; board-CEO/staff relationships; key CEO jobs, staff treatment, evaluations; and CEO parameters. They provided a template with specific language that nonprofits could use in adopting a BPM. SAF adapted most of those suggestions and added some of their own. These

BPM policies addressed the merits of a strong CEO or Board, cooperation/ autonomy among the CEO and the Board; finances; staff; and other factors.

When I first read the SAF BPM document in late 2015, and read Laughlin and Andringa later that year, I was impressed with the power of the BPM approach to crystallize the missions and responsibilities of an NGO. It clearly provided a means to foster open and transparent discussions about nonprofit governance and finances. The brand-new SAF BPM was well written and made the various components and responsibilities of the governing Board and the CEO explicit. Laughlin and Andringa stressed that a BPM reflects the relative power of a CEO and a Board in setting and implementing policies, and the SAF document did just that. In November 2015, I met the new CEO and commented on how impressed I was with the BPM that he had initiated at SAF (Society of American Foresters 2015)., with the foresighted caveat: if it were used seriously and updated as needed.

NGO Challenges

Almost all NGOs face challenges and debates about how to provide member services and attract more members, how to stay within a balanced annual operating budget, and Board/CEO/staff lines of authority. Maintaining adequate salary and operating budgets is a constant problem for most nonprofit interest groups (Peterson and Walker 1986). A primary goal of nonprofit organizations is to break even or better and not lose large sums of money. Small nonprofits often have problems obtaining funds and balancing annual budgets but could run some deficits if there were adequate reserve funds available. This is challenging in an era where all professional organizations have difficulty in attracting young members, as do social, environmental, or religious organizations (Sladek 2011). This background of a less-committed population creates difficulty for all modern volunteer organizations.

There are at least two polar views of solving this membership and organizational sustainability issue. The first view advocates investing (spending) funds on new staff and programs (e.g., membership, public relations, fundraising/development) to attract new members and retain old ones. In this respect, NGO leaders are similar to university leaders and probably private firms: larger staff will in theory pay off with better programs, more members, and more revenue than they cost. Supervising more employees also is often a HR criterion or bargaining chip for higher position grades and salaries. The other end of the spectrum is to balance the budget by reducing programs and staff as needed and accepting some attrition in the reach of a nonprofit organization. This approach requires tough choices by cutting programs and services that lose lots of money and seeking new lower-cost opportunities to accomplish the organization's mission.

Most senior administrators, of course, prefer spending funds and getting more staff on the premise of building programs. Charismatic con men may serve themselves with great promises of appealing program and staff investments with the promise to help carry an organization into better times. Patient leaders align mission, actions, and resources within the current operating budgets and hope that committed staff and high-quality program delivery can build programs that are enduring.

In traditional natural resource disciplines, the number of graduating students is less than in the past (Sharik et al. 2015), and the retirement of older members decreases paying membership and revenue. So it requires budget hawks to take the second strategy of budgets first, focus on core programs, and seize small wins as possible to help some organizations remain sustainable and survive. SAF was a model of this debate, with the CEO promoting great new programs and a large staff, at great cost, but with some disenchantment setting in as large expenses continued and the number of paying (not free retired or cheap student) memberships declined. There also are inherent issues in any NGO with CEO autonomy and line authority for hiring, firing, and directing the staff, versus board members thinking that the staff works for them and asking for a lot of their time.

SAF did indeed have problems that reflected these general issues of an NGO. They had sold part of their historic estate in Bethesda Maryland for a relative windfall of $16.5 million in 2014 and 2015 and proceeded to spend more than $4 million of that by the end of 2015, with little if anything to show for it, other than a new imperfect computer management information system and various management consulting analyses. The CEO instituted a policy in the BPM favoring his autonomy, which stated: "While the board's job is generally confined to establishing high-level policies, implementation and subsidiary policy development are delegated to the CEO. The key principle is, 'Staff Led; Board Governed'" (Society of American Foresters 2015).

More Issues Appear

When I arrived as Vice-President, I felt that we were on the wrong financial and governance track and had to intuitively develop a strategy for organizational change. Of course, I had to first reflect and (re)affirm that my values of budget discipline and Board fiscal responsibility and board member prerogatives were primary. I also had to find like-minded allies or give up. It, of course, seems hard to preach fiscal discipline in the Washington, DC, environment, and SAF with new large land sale financial reserves was no exception.

The current and past Presidents on the Board were more optimistic about the CEO leading and investing successfully for the future than the need for balancing budgets, and displeased with my opposition. But that is what Boards are supposed to do—debate and resolve organizational missions, directions, problems, and management. All organizations have these issues, and productive boards will identify, address, and improve problems continually in their leadership role. The SAF Board did work respectfully as professionals, and the past President was crucial during my presidency in the next year as major decisions continued to be made. His priorities as President in my first year largely did prevail, and I lost every vote we had about budgets that year and perhaps was the only person who voted to oppose the proposed million-dollar budget deficit. It was a tough first year on the Board.

As incoming Vice-President for 2016, at the first SAF board member training session in December 2015, I mostly listened to how this new Board worked and the responsibilities of Board Representatives and Officers. However, I did sense some uncertainty in how the new Board and new CEO relationships were working and complete confusion by everyone about the annual budget process and data. In the post-meeting round-robin comments at the end of the first Board meeting in 2015, I presciently commented that "[w]e need more budget clarity, transparency, and discipline." These issues were paramount, and my eventually successful goal was to reform the financial chaos during my 3-year tenure.

During my first year, as Vice-President, I chaired the Governance Committee, which had oversight for the Board policies, and sat on the Executive Committee, which set the Board's agenda and meetings. By the time the first of three SAF Board meetings occurred in 2016, I perceived a number of problems with our governance, management, and fiscal responsibility. Specifically, it appeared that we were spending almost $4 million per year, while revenues were $3 million per year. This left us with a ~$1 million operating deficit, although the budget statements provided to the Board did not actually calculate or show a net profit or loss, since it mixed withdrawals from our reserve funds with operating revenues to show only a "balanced" budget. The CEO also explicitly refused to provide the Board with budget details on staff salaries or contracts, which he said were his prerogative, not ours. Overall, budget revenue, expense, and withdrawals data from reserves remained opaque.

Other management problems seemed apparent to me, albeit not so much to others. About half the staff had retired or resigned in the last 2 years; accurate paid versus complimentary membership data were impossible to get from the staff; and while some board members had very good relations with the CEO, others, including me, were "ghosted." I was contacted by, called, or met with most of the departed staff, many of whom were friends from my previous 15 years as a SAF volunteer. They were even-handed but felt intimidated or humiliated by the CEO, which caused retirements or new jobs elsewhere. In addition, our best policies manual appropriately said that we had to ask the CEO for requests from the staff—who many of us had worked with on technical committees for at least a decade—but the CEO did not permit them to work on or even reply to our requests. So the staff were uncomfortable as well.

However, the CEO and current and past presidents interacted well, and I was an outsider. So, all of a sudden, this friendly nonprofit job had numerous issues. Volunteer management was no easier nor fulfilling than regular employment, and the lack of "line" authority and a 17-member Board of Directors made governance even more difficult than in a real job. Such frustrations often are the case, even as a volunteer or officer with conservation NGOs, charities, local governments, and many other volunteer organizations.

In response to my initial minority status, I worked to build support on the Board and with the grassroots members. Several board members were sympathetic old friends from my prior SAF technical committees and my jobs in our multi-state region. At social discussions after the Board meetings, some other persons also expressed concern about our fiduciary responsibilities and abrupt staff departures.

Part of my job as President-Elect and as President was to visit chapters across the country, and in those first 2 years I went to about ten and presented my "state of the union" talk, which included the apparent deficit spending data and issues, and I talked offline with local leaders about their views. I also networked actively at breaks, meals, and receptions and went on field trips at these meetings and engaged in fun conversations about forestry, which we all were there for, as well as in side conversations about local and national SAF membership and organizational issues. The national budget issues struck a chord with the conservative SAF grassroots leaders and members, who then usually lobbied their regional board members to protect our reserves and for balanced budgets.

Board Policies to Reflect Vision

In order to discuss the issues that I perceived, a transparent and open Board discussion again seemed to be the best tool available. If I were the only one who perceived that the management problems were severe, I would not be able to change the status quo, and I did not know where others stood. So I tried to get the issues out in the open. That way, win, lose, or draw, at least we would determine where SAF should go. It was scary to be apparently the only person who thought things were amiss. Past boards and leaders had developed the paths we were taking, so current members might be loath to recognize faults or change the status quo.

However, the SAF Governance Committee that I chaired as Vice-President in my first year dealt with strategic planning. I proposed that the Governance Committee also be responsible for maintaining and revising the new SAF BPM. As noted, the BPM provided an excellent vehicle to promote open discussion about values, roles, governance, and issues—it fostered reflection and open political discussions. In essence, the planning function that I started early in my government line positions was replaced by having an operational policy discussion through the BPM at SAF. In brief, my goals reflected the approaches discussed in Chapter 5—be open and transparent, treat staff well, have good cooperation between the CEO and Board, and begin to have fiscal discipline. I also foresaw that we could use the BPM measures as eventual KPIs to evaluate success of the CEO and the Board.

First, I had to get the full Board to approve that the Governance Committee had authority to change the BPM standards and that the BPM should be dynamic and changed often and easily. This was opposed by the CEO and others, who liked the current version slanted toward CEO authority and stasis. My motion for the Governance Committee to lead in proposing changes to the BPM (see #1.6 in Table 6.2) was defeated at the first Board meeting, but eventually the Governance Committee was authorized to propose changes at the next meeting, and we then proceeded apace to do so.

We had lively discussions as I proposed many revisions to the BPM at every meeting over the next 2 years. I proposed separate BPM amendments or new standards for fair staff treatment, CEO and Board governance, transparency, and required at least calculating a balanced operating budget, if not achieving one, as noted in Table 6.2. Other board members and committees also proposed amendments and additions, including a diversity and inclusion policy. These proposals wound their way through the relevant Board Committee, to the Executive Committee, and to a full Board vote if approved by each subordinate committee. All were vetted well in the committees before coming to the floor for Board consideration and passed with some modifications and general assent most of the time.

In addition to fomenting such debates, when I became President in the next year, I appointed Finance, Audit, Governance, and Executive Committee chairs and members that I thought would agree more with my board governance and views advocating our fiduciary responsibility for balanced budgets and energized the Board to be more hands-on and hold the CEO accountable. My mantra as President specifically followed the reasoning and quote from the Washington state forest practice act court decision, taken

Table 6.2 Selected changes in the Society of American Foresters Board Policies Manual from 2015 to 2017 (Society of American Foresters 2019)

BPM number	Revised SAF BPM as of 2017
1.1 Reasons for Adoption	Encouraging open, transparent, flexible, and **inclusive organizational decision making.**
1.6 Oversight Responsibility	The **Governance Committee will provide oversight and periodic review** of the Board Policies Manual and request suggestions for revision of board policies from Board committees or individual Board members. . . . . Note that the words are "primarily responsible" for drafting and reviewing those parts. There are no restrictions on who may propose modifications to the BPM—or draft specific language for that matter. **A well-integrated Board and BPM process will prompt frequent changes in the BPM.**
3.1 Governing Style	. . . The board is expected to foster a collaborative and cooperative organization that promotes discussion of goals, issues, opportunities, and solutions in an open, transparent, and collegial manner. The board is expected to provide a broad vision for SAF; ensure that its organizational structure can complete the tasks well; ensure programmatic and fiscal integrity; and represent the interests of the members, stakeholders, and beneficiaries. . . .
3.1.4	The **Board initiates policy,** not merely reacts to staff initiatives.
3.1.5	The Board fulfills its **fiduciary and legal responsibilities as a fundamental requirement** so it can focus on its commitment to keep its actions at a strategic level.
3.2.5 Board Job Description*	Encourage **open communication** among the board, members, and the CEO to foster continuous improvement and better programs.
3.7 Standing Board Committees	. . . Board **committees and staff should work together** to advance the mission and programs of SAF, but committees do not exercise line authority over staff.

3.7.2. Finance Committee	. . . Consistent with this responsibility, **it shall review the annual budget and reserve funds.** It shall review new planned major expenses whenever additional budget authority is requested by the CEO. Based on its budget review, the Finance Committee will submit the annual operating budget and reserve funds statement to the board for its approval. **The committee shall ensure that projected annual operating revenues meet or exceed annual expenses**, or if that is not the case, recommend any specific transfers from reserves and/or reserve interest income to the annual operating budget, and if there are any specific requirements to pay back those reserve funds. . . .
3.7.4* Executive Committee	In addition, the Executive Committee **shall conduct the initial annual evaluation of the CEO**, and report that evaluation to the full board for final action in an executive session without staff or the CEO, and meets with the CEO in executive session to discuss the evaluation. The Executive Committee will also draft the initial CEO Key Performance Indicators (KPIs) for the next fiscal year for approval by the full board. . . .
4.1 Delegation to the Chief Executive Officer (CEO)	The board's job is to represent all members of SAF and the professions of forestry and natural resources. This will involve a mix of strategic and tactical questions, both in selecting the resources and tradeoffs required to achieve these goals; and communicating with the CEO, staff, and members about priorities. **The CEO is the person with executive authority below the full board. He or she receives their authority from and is directly accountable to the Board as a whole.**
Delegation to CEO	4.2.3 **The board may change** its policies during any meeting, thereby shifting **the boundary between board and CEO domains.** Consequently, the board may change the latitude of choice given to the CEO, but so long as any particular delegation is in place, the board and its members will respect and support the CEO's choices. This does not prevent the board from obtaining information in the delegated areas. **The Executive Committee can obtain any line item budget details for current and past years, including, but not limited to, individual salaries, contracts, and fringes, which will be held confidential.** Staff names will not be associated with salary lists.
	4.2.4 **Board committee chairs and officers may make reasonable requests for information and expect to receive a reply** within two weeks, or some longer period as agreed upon by the requesting committee chair or officer and the CEO. . . . [If] in the CEO's judgment, [the request] requires excessive staff time or funds, it may be refused declined with an written explanation.
4.4 Staff Evaluations*	Each year before the review, the SAF staff will participate in a **360 evaluation** performance to provide feedback on the CEO.

(*Continued*)

Table 6.2 (Continued)

BPM number	Revised SAF BPM as of 2017
4.5 Annual Performance Review [4.6 in New BPMs]	The board **Executive Committee shall formally evaluate the CEO in executive session** . . . After meeting with the CEO, the Executive Committee will report on its review to the board in executive session, including recommendations on the CEO's compensation, which the board will then act upon.
4.7 Staff Treatment	The **CEO will treat staff and volunteers with professionalism**, respect, and courtesy. The CEO must work with staff members to refine a job description to direct their work, and the CEO must approve the final job description. The CEO must ensure that a employee grievance process is available. . .
5. Executive Parameters 5.2.1 Budgeting.	The budget during any fiscal period shall not (a) deviate materially from the board's goals and priorities listed in Part 2, (b) risk fiscal jeopardy, or (c) fail to show a generally acceptable level of foresight. In every budget year, **the CEO will submit to the Finance Committee and the board for consideration: (1) a balanced budget based only on the use of anticipated PROGRAM annual revenues and expenses; and (2) if necessary, a planned annual budget that has annual expenses that exceed annual revenues** with a specific request for any withdrawals or transfers from reserve funds or other sources.
5.2 Financial Controls	[The **CEO may not**] . . . 5.2.2.2 **Approve any major** expenditure or commitment without bringing a recommendation to the Finance Committee for approval through normal board procedure. 5.2.1.3 [**Approve any a budget that**] [**a**]**nticipates reducing current assets at year-end to less than the floor** established in the SAF Financial Reserve Policy or does not clearly state what the current Reserve balance, floor, and ceiling are.
5.6 Transparency*	5.6 **Transparency.** The CEO will ensure that governance and financial information is available to the membership and the public. 5.6.1 The following information will be posted to the **SAF public website** including: . . .
6.2 Diversity and Inclusion*	6.2 **Diversity and Inclusion.** The Society of American Foresters is committed to diversity and inclusion in our leadership, membership, programs, and activities. . .

(My **bold** wording to highlight key content; an * indicates a new BPM standard.)

from Edmund Burke. In I used that quote shown in Chapter 5 as a slide in every SAF Society or Board meeting talk that I made for 3 years.

I promoted an open, transparent, sustainable organization in every Board meeting talk I made, which was an implicit spin-off of the Collins (2001) *Good to Great* thesis. I lobbied the Board and the CEO continually for a balanced operating budget, to protect our land sale reserves and meet our fiduciary responsibilities. I argued that the best thing we could do for future foresters was to give them more money in our reserves to work with, which would yield more income from investments, and was much better then expensive new programs that did not pay off.

This repetition of the vision and key goals again followed the counsel of Block, and it slowly made an impression with the Board, if not the assent of the CEO. At times I overstated the importance of balancing operating budgets as a bargaining tactic, because we could use investment proceeds from the reserves if done wisely, but million-dollar deficits, consuming a great deal of reserves principal as well as interest, and unchecked spending were disastrous. As a forest economist, I also warned continually that the stock market could crash and inserted slides in my stump speeches with cover pages of *Fortune* and *The Economist* that projected just that. Major Bear markets downturns have not occurred yet, but negative returns did occur in 2018.

My fiscal pessimism at least, as well as maybe my focus on blocking and tackling and good personnel management, led my successor as President to often call me the Grim Reaper in our Board meetings, and surely not all the board members or many of the staff agreed with me on constrained budgets, although other transparency, staff treatment, responsiveness to Board requests of staff, and diversity goals were well received. Responding to the multiple fiscal, Board, and staff issues at SAF ended up being a 3-year-long slog.

For illustration, Table 6.2 summarizes about 18 of the 35 changes that I largely proposed to institute new SAF BPM policies (Society of American Foresters 2019), which were then sent to and debated and modified first by the relevant Board Committee of three persons and usually then considered and ratified by the full Board. Since one-third of the Board was elected and replaced every year, the Board politics and discussions were dynamic. But over my 3 years of leadership on the Board, more authority was assumed by the Board; more budget transparency and discipline did occur; accurate membership numbers and staff salary data were released to the Board; and treatment and evaluations of the staff improved. Also, the KPI metrics from the revised BPM fostered more constructive and formative evaluations of the CEO and for the Board.

The BPM and other discussions prompted the organization to reduce its operating budget deficit from $1.1 million in 2016 to $0.4 million in 2017 to $0.1 million in 2018. A transparency BPM was passed, and an understandable budget and all the Board meeting minutes were posted on the web, for all members to see. Other Board prerogatives were strengthened, and staff rights clarified. The CEO did not meet the new KPIs very well and was not satisfied with our new regime and BPM and left late in 2017, and a new CEO was hired and began in 2018.

The Next Regime

As is typical with regularly rotating Boards and representative democracy, my influence as past President waned in 2018 as new members and new CEO arrived. The BPM requiring the calculation of a balanced operating budget was rescinded in a close vote. This reflects the continual shifts in governance philosophy that occur in nonprofits as some line officers revolve each year. This is a characteristic of Board and officer "term limits." Just as I had fomented more Board governance and fiscal control as a new guy in 2016, to the chagrin of the President then, new members and the new CEO wanted to see programs and staff expand again in 2018, to my chagrin. That is the way democracy and majority rule in NGOs and governance often work and a reason that CEOs who last can often shape policies and practices more than transient Boards.

Like most NGOs in natural resources and conservation, SAF still will struggle with being a sustainable organization, balancing its operating budgets, and maintaining membership. Nonetheless, its policies as reflected in its BPM will focus on much more open and transparent governance, budget scrutiny, board responsibilities, and member service than before my perilous 3-year tenure as a SAF officer began, and hopefully more constructive Board/CEO/staff interactions will continue.

References

Block P. 1987. *The Empowered Manager: Positive Political Skills at Work.* San Francisco (CA): Jossey-Bass Publishers. 214 p.

Covey SR. 1990. *Principle-Centered Leadership.* New York: Free Press. 335 p.

Cubbage F, O'Laughlin J, Peterson N. 2017. *Natural Resource Policy.* Long Grove (IL): Waveland Press. 505 p.

Cubbage FW, McGinley KA. 2020. Chapter 7: Programs, services and other resources supporting the sustainable management of forests (Indicator 50). p. 117–124. In: Gen. Tech. Rep. IITF-GTR-52. Rio Piedras, PR: U.S. Department of Agriculture, Forest Service, International Institute of Tropical Forestry. 174 p.

Gordon JC, Berry JK. 2006. *Environmental Leadership Equals Essential Leadership: Redefining Who Leads and How.* New Haven (CT): Yale University Press. 164 p.

Gorte RW, Vincent CH, Hanson LA, Rosenblum MR. 2012. Federal land ownership: Overview and data. Washington (DC): Congressional Research Service 7–5700, R42436, 24 p.

Laughlin FL, Andringa RC. 2007. *Good Governance for Nonprofits.* New York: American Management Association. 210 p.

Peterson MA, Walker JL. 1986. Interest group responses to partisan change: the impact of Reagan administration upon the national interest group system. Pp. 162–182. In: Cigler, AJ, Loomis BA, (eds), *Interest Group Politics, 2nd* ed. Washington (DC): Congressional Quarterly.

Roosevelt T. 1910. Citizenship in a Republic. Speech Given at the Sorbonne in Paris on April 23, 1910. The speech is popularly known as "The Man in the Arena." Available at: www.theodorerooseveltcenter.org/Learn-About-TR/TR-Encyclopedia/Culture-and-Society/Man-in-the-Arena.aspx. Accessed 22 February 2020.

Sharik TL, Lilieholm RJ, Lindquist W, Richardson WW. 2015. Undergraduate enrollment in natural resource programs in the United States: trends, drivers, and implications for the future of natural resource professions. *J. Forestry,* 113(6): 538–551.

Sladek SL. 2011. *The End of Membership as We Know It.* Washington (DC): ASAE: The Center for Association Leadership. 122 p.

Society of American Foresters (SAF). 2015. Board Policies Manual (BPM) for the Society of American Foresters. This version of the BPM was approved by the board on May 30, 2015, v1–1 05302015. Available from SAF archives, Washington, DC, and from author files.

Society of American Foresters. 2019. Board Policies Manual (BPM) for the Society of American Foresters. This version of the BPM was approved by the board on May 5, 2019, v 5.0. Available at: www.eforester.org/Main/Community/Elected_Leadership/Main/Community/National_Elections.aspx?hkey=5044432e-fd7b-41ac-8013-d15dcff5f4f5. Accessed 22 February 2020.

Xu J. 2020. The review of humorous leader. *Open Journal of Business and Management* 8:542–551.

7 Environmental Activism to Stop the Hofmann Forest Sale

The Proposed Hofmann Forest Sale

This third current case recounts the story of the 2013 NC State University proposed sale of the 79,000 acre Hofmann Forest—a deep pocosin swamp on the North Carolina coast. This case is similar to frequent development versus environmental protection decisions, only at scale at least 100 times as large, and with much greater potential long-term adverse impacts. The NC State University Natural Resource Foundation offered the sale, despite its education, research, extension missions. Julius Hofmann, the first director of the School of Forestry, had acquired the property in 1934, financed it with long-term bonds, and set up a separate Forestry Foundation to manage it. Over the next eight decades, the foundation managed the forest for education and research, as well as income from timber sales and hunting leases.

The Hofmann Forest is a deep pocosin swamp, and much of it has been drained and managed with an extensive system of major ditches and lateral minor ditches. Ditching was legal at the time in the 1960s and early 1970s, before the 1972 Clean Water Act and Section 404 wetland dredge and fill permit regulations. By 2013, the Hofmann was managed intensively, with 55,000 acres converted to pine plantations and 24,000 acres of deep swamps, and it was the crown jewel of our approximately ten forest holdings. The Hofmann has immense wildlife, biodiversity, water quality, and environmental values as well as timber and hunting outputs. It provides a wildlife corridor between nearby state game lands and a national forest and is full of bear, deer, and turkey, and nongame species and rare plants. It is the partial fount of three rivers that run to the nearby coast and bays, helping protect downstream shellfish and nearby beach water quality. Its high ground near Jacksonville could be developed, and its ditched and drained wet swamps could be converted to row crops at least in theory.

DOI: 10.4324/9781003141297-7

Leadership and Activism

The proposed sale of the Hofmann instantly triggered huge opposition from the public, forestry and natural resource alumni, wildlife and environmental groups, and the media, among others. It quickly prompted me and other faculty, forestry alumni, and new environmental friends to mobilize opposition and pursue all possible internal and external means to stop the sale. Many faculty, some students, a key environmental leader, locals by the forest, and a host of other stakeholders coalesced to oppose the sale.

Leadership in activism constitutes demonstrating personal or collective values in the pursuit of environmental or social change. The "context" for activism is less clearly defined than the role of government or nonprofit organizations and often is focused on social or environmental issues, involving power relations between elected or appointed decision-makers and unofficial opponents, and includes a variety of strategies and tactics used by participants in a policy issue. While there are many activist ENGOs, or even ad hoc citizen groups that often are formed to fight excessive development or promote nature conservation, it takes many participants to actually change any public policy, since those policies usually are developed by vested interests and official decision makers.

Furthermore, as an activist, you have none of the formal authority of a line manager or even the elected line authority of a nonprofit board member. You are simply trying to organize a loose coalition of interested persons and groups, usually to lead to environmental or social change. You still might have clear goals—such as stop toxic water pollution, save a forest from development, decrease global climate change—but other public and private sectors control the resources and make the decisions about the importance of achieving such goals. Thus, you must try various strategies and tactics. You may be able to measure success, by improving environmental quality, preventing land development or pollution, helping propose and enact laws or change regulations, or other metrics. But slow progress or even prevention of worse environmental damage is hard to measure. That has by no means diminished environmental efforts, but the context for success and continued efforts rests far more on values and beliefs than on a bottom line.

A number of pithy quotes illustrate activism:

> To sit home, read one's favorite paper, and scoff at the misdeeds of the men who do things is easy, but it is markedly ineffective. It is what evil men count upon the good men doing.
> —Theodore Roosevelt (1895)

> Most activism is brought about by us ordinary people.
> —Patricia Hill Collins (2020)

[I]n long intervals I have expressed an opinion on public issues when-ever they appeared to me so bad and unfortunate that silence would have made me feel guilty of complicity.

—Albert Einstein (1954)

The preceding quotes illustrate the importance of activism and, like many popularized citations, bear some examination. Roosevelt's is classic, accepted, and among his most cited. The one from Patricia Collins, an African American sociologist, is even more popular on the web for posters but not really possible to find in print as an original quote. The quote from Einstein, who opposed Nazism and Jim Crow laws, is usually expressed as a more widely recognized quote on the web of "If I were to remain silent, I'd be guilty of complicity." But it is not possible to find that popular quote. Nonetheless, the fuller version provides a more interesting insight into activism—it represents only how he felt, and activism is an exercise of volition used infrequently or sparingly and for major issues, not exercised for daily slights and insults (Olsen 2020).

Recently in my career, I have become more of an activist, branching from my professional interests. I have always supported professional organizations and forest landowner associations by being a member and a leader, as noted. This expanded with mostly passive support as a member and financial contributor for a dozen or more forestry, conservation, environmental organizations (ENGOs) in the last few decades. I also have written op-eds in the Raleigh News and Observer and the NC State student paper, the *Technician*. These op-eds have included utilitarian advocacy for forestry and wood use (e.g., bioenergy and wood frame housing), environmental advocacy for protecting our natural resource patrimony (opposing ruthless state environmental deregulation), and social commentaries against racism and for vaccines. Letters to the editor often reflect efforts to change the status quo, which are not easy to achieve, and do confront opinions of established interests, so bear some risks.

The Sale Is Announced

NC State University and the College of Natural Resources announced the Hofmann Forest sale publicly on January 23, 2013. This group was named the Forestry Foundation when formed by Hofmann in 1929 and then reorganized as the Natural Resource Foundation in 2008, which seems to have been a purposeful precursor to selling the Hofmann, since the various forestry members and locals by the Hofmann were all removed from the Board within a few years.

The context for me here was unusual when I quickly decided to oppose the sale, akin to that of a whistleblower. Whistleblowers oppose apparently bad practices and policies of organizations that they work for, and when unsuccessful at changing them from within, try to reverse them via public exposure and government assistance. This is a last resort when working from within has failed, but a person feels deeply that a dire situation requires a large personal risk to protect the public interest.

Unfortunately, whistleblowers have a hard time, which might be described as follows: expose an illicit action, often by your own employer; fight for public help to halt the action; generate ill will and acrimony from bosses and perhaps peers in your organization; improve the situation if fortunate and well received externally; usually suffer marginalization and reprisal whether successful or not; but garner personal satisfaction and some external praise for doing the right thing. The Hofmann sale opponents risked this fate, but I literally remembered the preceding quote about activism by TR from my youth and felt that the gross mistake of the sale warranted action.

The Natural Resources Foundation and our College Dean announced the sale of the Hofmann in its entirety and stated that the income from the sale (perhaps more than $100 million) would provide more financial assistance for our natural resource students than having the foundation and college managing a commercial forest. The Dean announced on the web and to the college in an email (Watzin 2013):

> The College is currently experiencing significant growth and has strong ambitions. Keeping current programs strong and leveraging new opportunities for the College will only be possible with additional cash flow. A more diversified portfolio of investment could provide a higher and more consistent level of support to the College . . . The current rate of return from the Hofmann is less than what might be achieved from a diversified investment portfolio. A diversified portfolio would also lessen the risks associated with fires, hurricanes, droughts, and invasive species.

This proposed sale shocked a large amount of forestry alumni and the environmental community and prompted major public, faculty, and student opposition to the sale. I had some affinity for the Hofmann after serving as Department Head for 10 years, and working with the old Forestry Foundation and the attending annual forest tour and barbeque with local community members at the forest during Forestry Foundation meetings, and had worked with faculty who taught and conducted research there. Furthermore, the Hofmann was the epitome of what we taught in our forestry, wildlife, and natural resources majors, allowing us to indeed practice what we teach—sustainable forest management—at an immense scale. Selling the Hofmann after 80 years of ownership to invest in Wall Street seemed to be the antithesis of why a College of Natural Resources and Department of Forestry and Environmental Resources existed.

The sale betrayed the education and sustainable management vision that taught as teachers and natural resource professionals. Furthermore, the secret process of preparing the sale betrayed the transparency, openness, and stakeholder consultation that we profess. In fact, even if a sale were considered, we could have had our students prepare environmental assessments (EAs) of its proposed impacts, which we teach as well. So ultimately, the sale revealed that the university was forsaking its core missions of teaching and research about natural resources management for its obtusely stated mission of increasing its funds and budgets, purportedly to help students and faculty. This surely was not aligning resources and actions with our stated intentions.

Hofmann Sale Opposition Mounts

In response to this infidelity to our real mission, starting initially with about ten faculty and some students, we opposed the sale. However, input was discouraged and faculty felt threatened by the possibility of adverse effects on future raises and research support, so as the process ground on many of the faculty desisted. Our official power as faculty and ENGOs was minimal, and the Natural Resource Foundation, the College of Natural Resources, and the university pursued the sale resolutely. They also withheld all relevant information about the sale, claiming that the Natural Resource Foundation (which was housed above the Dean's office) was a private organization and therefore not subject to state open meeting or records laws, nor was the Dean when acting as a board member of the foundation. Despite the private organization shield, the Dean and Chancellor spoke and wrote aggressively on behalf of the sale; the university public relations office periodically issued glowing press releases and newspaper articles touting the merits of the sale; and eventually the university and state lawyers handled most of an eventual lawsuit against the sale.

In communicating about the sale with the faculty, the Natural Resource Foundation Director and the Dean staged a few pro-forma meetings with faculty where no notes or follow-up actions were taken. They inferred that any sale would include a conservation easement to protect the land and would only sell the timber rights. However, in the final sale announcement, they ultimately revealed that the sale would include the entire forest and land and rebuffed all our attempts as faculty, alumni, environmental groups, and other stakeholders to stop the sale, using what has been termed a "decide-announce-and-defend" strategy in the academic literature (Hendry 2004).

Clearly, a much broader and extensive response was required to halt the proposed sale. The strategy needed to be far different than that of a line manager, who had institutional authority to make a decision, or an NGO board member who had at least soft power to do so. Our efforts with faculty, students, and foresters to stop the sale were invigorated greatly when Ron Sutherland of the Wildlands Network joined as a coleader of the opposition, bringing great vision and vast wildlife and environmental contacts to the fray. Sutherland recognized and promoted the crucial importance of the Hofmann as a coastal wildlife corridor and refuge for flora and fauna and brought innovative and photogenic public relations ideas—protests, street signs, hundreds of pine seedlings in cups, a white horse at a protest—and technical GIS and web site skills. He also wrote editorials, posted on all newspaper and environmental blogs, and recruited activist environmental groups to the cause.

As activists, we intuitively opted for an issue expansion strategy that we were familiar with, such as described by Cobb and Elder (1972), and tried various tactics to oppose the sale. *Our eventual key vision and objectives for our activist campaign were to try to stop the sale, get foresters and locals reappointed to the Natural Resource Foundation Board, and protect the Hofmann Forest with a conservation easement.* We campaigned tirelessly to expand the Hofmann sale issue and foster more opposition and publicity so that the university would reverse its misguided decision.

Our ultimate informal opposition leadership group consisted of me, Joe Roise as another faculty member, Ron Sutherland, one savvy undergraduate student leader from the College of Humanities, and a couple of local leaders who lived near the Hofmann Forest. The sale was such a bad idea that we also had many people volunteering to help us in any way during the 2-year debate. This included actively engaged students, foresters, many media representatives, activists from other environmental campaigns, local citizens by the Hofmann, several loyal and influential alumni from the College of Natural Resources and from the College of Agriculture, some anonymous forestry faculty, and a few anonymous business leaders in North Carolina. They provided very useful help in promoting the issue—publishing favorable articles, sending notices to their listservs, contacting NC State Board of Trustees members, speaking with university administrators, speaking at protests, and more. All of the volunteers agreed that the idea of selling the forest was wrong at a variety of levels and definitely should be stopped.

We started our conservation campaign with internal efforts at NC State University and the College of Natural Resources, and the Natural Resource Foundation. Those internal efforts were always stonewalled by the university administration, so we expanded our efforts to the media, external stakeholders, and decision makers in the broader public and ultimately in the courts. Table 7.1 summarizes most, but not all, of the efforts we pursued to stop the sale.

******

Table 7.1   Spectrum of principal internal and external activist approaches used and outcomes to stop the Hofmann Forest sale

NCSU Internal Appeals and Opposition and Input—All Failed or Ignored in the Short Run

- Attended preliminary sale consideration "information" sessions and opposed any sale
- Responded to every NCSU press release and CNR email list when responses were allowed and not stopped by post-only format
- Developed a Department of Forestry Faculty opposition petition
- Developed a Department of Forestry student opposition petition
- Met with Dean and Forestry Foundation and University Foundation Leaders
- Requested meetings with Chancellor—no reply
- Submitted and approved a Department of Forestry Faculty opposition resolution
- Developed, submitted, and tried to present Faculty and Student Senate Resolutions to stop the sale—I was not allowed to speak at the Faculty Senate vote—both resolutions failed
- Wrote letters, memos, emails of opposition to Chancellor, Dean, NCSU Board of Trustees—No replies, ever
- Gave a token invited presentation in opposition at Natural Resource Foundation—which voted to sell the entire Forest immediately afterward in that meeting
- Made open records requests for sale details—some granted; some denied
- Prompted student/faculty/local community letters, protests, student newspaper articles

- Student organizer contacted the Student Senate and clubs; set up NCSU protests with request to Public Safety; contacted Board of Trustee members or friends; prompted an informal online NCSU student referendum on the sale, with ~80% voting to stop the sale.

External Opposition to Stop the Sale

- Created online petitions—two different sources; more than 12,000 total signatures, lots of insightful comments
- Created Hofmann Forest Facebook Page—about 4500 likes
- Created Hofmann Forest information and overview web site—many hits
- Printed and distributed 600 "Save Hofmann Forest" signs, surrounding most campus entrances, and spread across the Raleigh area and the Jacksonville/Hofmann region
- Encouraged letters to Dean, Chancellor, Natural Resource Board, and Alumni Foundation Director, and State Attorney General promoted by conservation organizations and their newsletters—more than 5000 emails and some letters at least sent to various decision makers
- Wrote many large opinion editorials published in local newspapers and in professional and trade magazines.
- Fostered newspaper articles—general newspaper articles in Raleigh, Charlotte, Jacksonville, and elsewhere—covered the Hofmann sale issue and eventual lawsuit extensively, not taking sides, but presenting the opposition view well; we talked to various reporters often, first in person and later by phone, and knew who covered the story in Raleigh
- Generated editorials in newspapers—newspaper editorial boards all across the state wrote about 15 editorials largely opposing the sale
- Wrote in blogs and responses—formal opponents and the public wrote scores to maybe hundreds of online comments on newspaper stories. At least 90% opposed the sale.
- Made public protests—always with custom signs, and usually with pine seedlings in plastic cups—at Chancellor's residence, NCSU Board of Governors, Natural Resource Foundation, Brickyard (Campus Common Area), and by Hofmann Forest. The press was invited to and a few often attended these.

- Suggested that alumni and donors contact the Natural Resource Foundation and University Endowments—many did stop cash gifts and some withdrew estate gifts
- Facilitated resolutions of opposition from two professional forestry organizations
- Led resolutions of opposition and Friends Letter from ~15 environmental groups
- Led active opposition from local groups by Hofmann Forest
- Filed a lawsuit based on Failure to File a State Environmental Impact Assessment
- Invited to talk on radio shows and appeared on a North Carolina Now TV show
- Appealed to friends, distinguished emeritus faculty, and friends of friends and business and government leaders, who did talk and intervene with Chancellor and Dean and asked them to change their decision

The extensive internal efforts all failed at the university level but did create lots of adverse publicity about the sale for the university, which helped expand the issue and keep it in the media. In his leadership book based on his almost two decades as a college president, Steven Sample (2002) writes a whole chapter about challenges with the press and the importance of a good public image. The proposed Hofmann sale generated immense negative press for the university for almost 2 years, which definitely harmed its image and presumably its fund-raising as well.

Unfortunately, these significant internal efforts and the external media and public relations campaign alone did not prompt the university, College of Natural Resources, and Natural Resources Foundation to change its complete sale goal or ever consult with any stakeholders or respond. However, the internal and external efforts clearly conveyed the unpopularity of the sale with the public, many forestry and natural resource alumni, and most faculty. The decision to sell was widely criticized in newspapers across the state, and the blog comments on those and other sources were almost universally opposed to the sale as forsaking our mission and values (Cubbage et al. 2016). As opponents, we received continual positive feedback for our efforts, from many extremely displeased stakeholders, many who said they were vocal in expressing their opinions to the Dean and to the Chancellor, and stopping or withdrawing their gifts and contributions to the university.

The sale was becoming a public relations disaster for NC State and the College of Natural Resources and, we heard, was adversely affecting contributions even in other colleges such as agriculture.

Environmental Lawsuit

Despite our media, interest group pressure, and moral progress, the university remained single-minded in its pursuit of a complete sale of the forest. So we sought and retained James Conner as our lawyer to file a lawsuit to stop the sale due to lack of preparing a state EA document (Cubbage, et al. vs. The Board of Trustees of the Endowment Fund of NC State University et al. 2014). Five purposefully diverse plaintiffs joined the lawsuit—Cubbage as a faculty member, Ron Sutherland as an ENGO staff member and wildlife scientist, Jim Gregory, a former faculty member and hydrologist for 50 years who had worked extensively on the Hofmann, Barny Bernard, a consulting forester who was a former Chairperson of the Forestry Foundation, and local landowner who lived near the Hofmann.

The choice to pursue a court case illustrates our leadership vision and tactics well. Sutherland and I saw very early that a lawsuit might be needed to stop the sale and independently talked to a few different lawyers for a few months about the prospects, as we pursued the other tactics mentioned in Table 7.1. In addition, in the previous months, I talked, visited, had coffee or lunch with, and discussed opposition ideas, including a lawsuit, to more than a dozen people who called me to express outrage at the sale. We identified many ways they could help and got their phone numbers and emails.

When we met with James Conner the first time, he stated that we needed to have Co-Plaintiffs who would be ready to sign on within a couple of days so we could file a preliminary injunction to stop the sale. We discussed our known prospects and chose the diverse group noted earlier, representing persons who had tangible, immediate, and personal interest in case, as required to be successful in "standing" to bring a lawsuit. Sutherland, Conner, and I called my prime contacts that afternoon from his law office and obtained three more willing co-plaintiffs. I signed a contract to hire Conner; he drafted an injunction and was ready to go within a day. One other local landowner dropped out, but our prior networking and contacts had us ready to file for equity relief—a preliminary injunction to stop the sale—within about three days.

The court challenge was a brave and scary tactic but again reflected the leadership and professional principles I espoused—teach what you believe and practice what you teach—sustainable forest management and advocacy for one's conservation beliefs. Indeed, I chose to practice my principles, serving as the lead plaintiff against the university, and signing a contract that

I would pay all the legal fees if necessary. In the end, more than 100 persons contributed large amounts anonymously to an account with the Wildlands Network for the legal costs, with some sending in up to $3,000 to $5,000 during the several months in court. These contributions covered about half of the eventual $60,000 in invoices, so my net expenses were reduced. This issue is typical for conservation versus development cases, where locals have to hold fund raisers and bake sales to contend with well-funded developers or university foundations and the state in this case.

As plaintiffs we had to prove that we had standing to bring such a lawsuit, that the Hofmann Forest was state land, that Natural Resource Foundation/ University Foundation holding the property title did not make it exempt as a quasi-private organization (recall the foundations are housed on university property, and it had offices near the Dean, university space, credit cards, and finance systems), and that the foundation/university was subject to the North Carolina Environmental Policy Act (SEPA) and failed to perform the state EA as required by SEPA.

The Hofmann Forest was owned in a purposefully opaque legal arrangement set up only three decades ago, explicitly to avoid paying county property taxes. The NCSU Endowment Fund holds the title as a quasi-public entity, but the forest was managed by the Natural Resource Foundation. Both claimed to be private nonprofit organizations in the lawsuit and thus exempt from the state SEPA (and the federal Endangered Species Act as well), and used the private basis to refuse all our state open records requests for any foundation minutes or decisions. Our attorney said this was not legal, but it would require a separate lawsuit, which we could not afford.

However, early on in the issue, I visited the local Jones County Tax Assessor who had old Hofmann tax debate files and found a 1980 letter from the State Attorney General that said specifically that the Hofmann Forest was state land and exempt from property taxes. Our lawyer then argued pretty successfully that as state land, the university would have to perform an EA and maybe an environmental impact assessment (EIS) before the sale (Cubbage et al. v. the Board of Trustees. . . 2014). Such a full state SEPA EIS was required to be 60 pages or less (CEQ 2020), and an EA could be only 30 pages long. However, the foundation and university instead spent hundreds of thousands of dollars and prepared hundreds of pages of legal documents to avoid the EA/EIS, perhaps suggesting that they knew well that the analysis of the sale's environmental impacts would not be positive or helpful for the sale.

Our lawyer James Conner and our case were excellent. Ironically, several attorneys from the State of North Carolina Attorney General's Office led the foundation/university team against our case, claiming dubiously and not very successfully that the Hofmann was not state land nor subject to the relevant state laws. The Natural Resource Foundation also hired two lawyers to help defend the SEPA lawsuit, and the university legal counsel also advised and attended the trials. So as is common, our modest environmental legal team and expenses were dwarfed by the deeper pockets of the development interests.

We went to trial and lost in a request for a preliminary injunction to the Wake County Court, because the judge stated that the sale was not "imminent"—there were not bulldozers at the gates—but he recommended the litigants read the *Lorax* by Dr. Seuss. We appealed and requested a temporary injunction and lost because a different judge stated that we had not proven that there would be irrevocable damage from a sale (this is not the purpose of an EA/EIS; it is to evaluate potential damage). We appealed that decision to the district North Carolina appellate court.

In a rare surprise move, which had not occurred in decades, the North Carolina Supreme Court reached down and took the case and several other major ones from the appellate court. However, when the initial sale to a farm bidder folded, the Supreme Court ruled the case moot, which meant neither side won, but a new case could be filed if we so chose. It is worth noting that in all of these trials, we were not disqualified for not having standing, nor was the Hofmann ruled to be private, although the quite brief written decisions were silent on both points. These neutral opinions, as well as the case being heard by the Supreme Court, indicate that our case surely had substantial merit, or it would not have gone so far.

Issue Outcomes

The Hofmann was initially contracted to be bought by a large farmer and family company from Illinois for $145 million. His prospectus for cutting down and developing the entire forest was leaked to us the day after the second trial. The plans included clear-cutting the entire planted forest, converting about 9,000 acres of the highest ground near the city of Jacksonville to a gated housing and golf community, and using most of the rest to farm corn and soy beans. Once that became known, public and ENGO opposition intensified, the court case and appeals proceeded to the North Carolina Supreme Court.

Meanwhile, an unknown whistleblower filed a complaint with the EPA for illegal ditching on the Hofmann, which was investigated. The Natural Resource Foundation was then prosecuted and fined by EPA and the Corps of Engineers for illegal draining of the swamp in the Hofmann Forest (NC Coastal Federation 2015; NC Policy Watch 2016). The furor of the opposition, threats of wetland violations and permit requirements stopping development of the Hofmann, and possible adverse impacts on other USDA crop payments, and decreased crop prices may have convinced the buyer to withdraw.

In the end, in 2015, NC State University and the College of Natural Resource leaders changed their thinking and approach in the face of such strong opposition and unremitting bad publicity for the university and the college. They decided that it would be better to retain the Hofmann Forest land as their property in the University Endowment and to make a timber deed sale for the rights to harvest trees and manage the Hofmann Forest.

A southern Timber Investment Management Organization (TIMO) that already managed a large amount of land in North Carolina made a successful offer of $78 million for a 50-year timber deed. That timber deed is now owned by a secret investor(s) elsewhere. The Natural Resource Foundation and NC State Endowment Fund still own the land, but the TIMO manages the property for profit for the investor. This contract essentially ended the public debate and effectively transferred management of the timber, and in reality, access to the property, to the TIMO and the secret investor for the next 50 years. The foundation retained an option to buy back about 9,000 acres of developable high ground but has not elected to do so and probably will not be given the expense and adverse publicity hazards that might entail.

The TIMO foresters are familiar colleagues, professional acquaintances, and leaders in SAF, also blunting our criticism and public opposition compared to a silent farm owner from Illinois. The foresters are friendly, welcome university student visits, maintain most prior research trials, and manage the forest well. They allow limited new university research use on request but keep the forest gated and closed to locals except hunt clubs that lease those rights. Per accepted law for private LLC corporations that TIMOs often use, the owner of the timber deed is still quite literally a state secret but receives the benefit of not paying any property taxes because the NCSU Endowment and Natural Resource Foundation have claimed the Hofmann is exempt as state land before and after the lawsuit, albeit not state land in court.

Per the previous whistleblower analogy, as opponents of our own organization's decision, we remained employed, but with some retribution. While direct causation is unprovable, the handful of senior faculty who opposed the sale received less research support and recognition for years, while selected colleagues that avoided the issue garnered some raises and some distinguished professor recognitions. Three of us as faculty opponents, albeit quite productive, received bad annual reviews and essentially no discretionary raises every year from 2014 to 2020 and were shunned by less outspoken colleagues. Perhaps by coincidence, I was fired as the codirector of our successful SOFAC economics co-op that I founded 25 years ago without any notice or explanation. Many forestry professors and staff who quietly opposed the sale left the university due to other uncontested job offers, early retirement, or partial loss of hard money salary support.

However, the professional security that we had due to tenure and our high levels of productivity and visibility gave us adequate employment protection so far. We did fulfill our commitment as leaders and pursued the right thing, helping the college achieve our real educational and research missions, albeit with a lifelong decrease in our salary and retirement income. I did receive many profound personal thanks from old and new professional friends, as well as several distinguished service awards and plaques for the Hofmann campaign efforts from the Appalachian Society of American Foresters, the North Carolina Association of Consulting Foresters, and the North Carolina Coastal Federation. The few other remaining active Hofmann opponents in the college did not even get those moral rewards unfortunately.

Funding and Missions

While the sale outcome advanced to a reasonable outcome after much contention, the university can no longer demonstrate that it can manage such a large forest, which is what we teach. Nor can we obtain any management data from the forest for teaching or research—such as timber growth rates, harvest schedules, planting and management cost, or timber sales information—as we had for the previous 80 years. We still do have and manage about 5,000 acres of other smaller forests well, but they do not provide information on an industrial size estate, and the other forests are located in the Piedmont, while the Hofmann is located in the Coastal Plain that is in the heart of the forest industry in North Carolina.

The Natural Resource Foundation and University received $78,046,107 as a lump sum payment for the timber deed sale effective July 1, 2016. It paid $1,017,665 in closing costs and withheld $7,056,426 for FY 2017–2018 spending and other assessments, leaving $69,963,016 for investments. The corpus of the investment generated about $2.7 million dollars of unrestricted funds per year to spend in FY 2019–2021. And by January 1, 2021, the principal in the investment fund was $85 million, a 21% increase not including the $8.2 million in annual withdrawals (Cook 2021). Including the withdrawals, the net return would be about 33%. This does sound impressive, but it is worth noting that the S&P 500 index during this same time increased 72.5% (Damodaran 2021), so the university sale corpus underperformed that benchmark by more than half.

Despite the windfall from the sale, its widely touted benefits to the faculty and students did not materialize as of the first 5 years. Since the sale, our previous 20+ years of individual faculty operating allocations were eliminated; student scholarships did not increase at all; and funding for our 20+ year successful professional Forestry and Environmental Education continuing education program was eliminated, forcing it to close and the two staff to leave. eight local persons who worked on the Hofmann Forest were fired and have been replaced by one employee with the TIMO, and one was retained with the foundation as an analyst.

The Hofmann sale increased the university and college unrestricted endowments by about $70 million and generated about $2.7 million per year, which was more than the ~$2 million it received by owning and managing the forest ourselves. So financially, one could argue that investing in stocks and bonds instead of owning and managing timber or a forest was better—provided that such investments are not adversely affected by stock market downturns or an enduring recession. The sale, however, did not demonstrate to our students or society why one should enter our professions and practice careers in natural resources.

There also might have been other ways than a sale for the university and foundation to increase income from the Hofmann by being leaders and innovating in sale of ecosystem services such as water storage and carbon storage, and they are currently negotiating for a 2,000 acre solar farm to replace agricultural lands there. Overall, the university played hardball against opponents during and after the sale and abandoned our College of Natural Resources and University visions of sustainability, professional natural resource management, and stakeholder consultation. And we have less operating funds in the Department of Forestry and Environmental Resources than we did before the Hofmann sale.

In the end, our enthusiastic coalition of academic, professional, citizen, local, environmental, and business activists helped prevent the sale of the Hofmann Forest lock, stock, and barrel. The Natural Resources Foundation now has foresters appointed on the Board. They even have started posting brief minutes from the foundation meetings on the web for transparency. We sought a conservation easement for the Hofmann. The timber deed is not quite that but may achieve the same effect for 50 years. But it still felt a little disappointing because we were stonewalled and never consulted or included during the process outside of the courtroom, and it did not build any long-term commitment to collaboration or dialogue, therefore falling short of what we teach. There still is essentially no local interaction as in the past and not much openness or diversity in the forest goods and services produced, which could be improved.

Our selected faculty, student, and allies' path of leadership in advocacy and activism in editorials, Hofmann Forest opposition, and occasional other public forums demonstrated commitment to fulfilling our conservation principles of sustainable forest management and natural resource management. These actions for me were filled with doubts and terror but stem from my enduring beliefs that were formed during my career in the core visions of our professions in sustainable development, coupled with fairness, transparency, and collegial governance.

Leadership Implications of the Three Cases

Hopefully my three management experiences described here in Chapters 6 and 7 provide useful illustrations of different ways one can be a leader. The cases are reasonably representative of line management in government, staff and elected officers in nonprofit, and activists in environmental campaigns. All of the examples from public, nonprofit, and activist domains provided in these two chapters were touchstones to our professional visions of sustainable development and management aligning organizational resources and intentions.

These examples suggest that all professionals involved in leadership, management, and activism need to have conviction and courage. Even when vision and intentions are aligned, problems, opposition, and self-doubt will occur. And even when managers and activists are confident that they are right and have a good team, pursuing change and reform of institutional policies and practices takes determination and prolonged persistence to change the status quo, culture, policy, and practice, and perhaps years for success, if ever.

The private sector is somewhat different, but the applications presented here apply there as well. Many of the books and articles in this and previous chapters draw from private sector management and leadership. I also have worked as a contractor with private firms as a consultant in economics and policy, for law firms, for forest products firms, for trade associations, and for the World Bank. They are even more driven by aligning the consulting task one performs with their mission and the work you are hired to do.

In the three major examples in these chapters, I identified or reaffirmed and promoted our research, education, professionalism, and conservation visions in each organization. That vision relates back to the actual sustainable development of the land and natural resources and carries over to the sustainability of each organization I led or co-led. I followed the management cycle presented in Figure 1.1 and used authentic and open strategies and tactics such as fairness and merit, transparency and communication and collaboration, monitoring and fair rewards, and assessment and improvement.

My leadership in some contentious issues did not necessarily help my career advance, at least in my preferred ideal family location in North

Carolina. Furthermore, candor and speaking truth to power instead of cautiously managing upward might have contributed to less advancement, which was cemented by leading an environmental lawsuit against my employer. C'est la vie.

Really, no one, including even the most famous leaders in the world, will achieve all the goals that they seek. Only a rare few of almost all ambitious persons will be able to be promoted as far as they might like. I will not retire in penury and usually made the right choices in aligning resource and actions with stated intentions and practicing what I teach, as a manager, as a professional, and as an activist. I learned, followed, practiced, and helped lead in our professional vision of sustainable development, natural resources stewardship, education, research, and outreach.

References

Cobb RW, Elder CD. 1972. *Participation in American politics: The Dynamics of Agenda-Building.* Baltimore (MD): Johns Hopkins University Press. 182 p.

Collins PH. 2020. Activism. Available at: www.brainyquote.com/quotes/patricia_hill_collins_531306. Accessed 22 February 2020.

Cook S. 2021. Hofmann sale and investment funds summary. College of Natural Resources Online Faculty Meeting. January 22, 2021.

Council on Environmental Quality (CEQ), Executive Office of the President of the United States. 2015. Introducing federal National Environmental Policy Act Practitioners to the North Carolina State Environmental Policy Act. 3p. Available at: https://ceq.doe.gov/docs/laws-regulations/state_information/NC_NEPA_Comparison_23Nov2015.pdf. Accessed 14 March 2020.

Cubbage F, Roise J, Sutherland R. 2016. The proposed sale of the Hofmann Forest: A case study in natural resource policy. In: *Forest Economics and Policy in a Changing Environment: How Market, Policy, and Climate Transformations Affect Forests.* Proceedings of the 2016 Meeting of the International Society of Forest Resource Economics. Forest Service Southern Research Station e-General Technical Report SRS-218, December 2016. Available at: http://sofew.cfr.msstate.edu/papers/cubbage16.pdf. Accessed 24 February 2017. p. 81–93.

Cubbage, Sutherland, Barnard, Gregory, Eddy vs. The Board of Trustees of the Endowment Fund of NC State University et al. 2014.772 S.E. 2d 855, 2014 N.C. LEXIS 1232 **; 367 N.C. 778.

Damodaran A. 2021. Historical returns on stocks, bonds and bills: 1928–2020. Available at: http://pages.stern.nyu.edu/~adamodar/New_Home_Page/datafile/histretSP.html. Accessed 16 February 2021.

Einstein A. 1954. [I]n long intervals I have expressed an opinion on public issues whenever they appeared to me so bad and unfortunate that silence would have made me feel guilty of complicity. Cited at: Olsen W. The Stupidest Einstein Meme. Commentary. Cato Institute. Available at: www.cato.org/publications/commentary/stupidest-einstein-meme. Accessed 22 February 2020.

Hendry J. 2004. Decide, announce, defend: Turning the NEPA process into an advocacy tool rather than a decision-making tool. In: Depoe SP, Delicath JW, Elsenbeer MFA, editors. *Communication and Public Participation in Environmental Decision Making.* Albany (NY): State University of New York Press. p. 99–112

NC Coastal Federation. 2015. Corps reports ditching violation in Hofmann. Available at: www.carolinacoastonline.com/tideland_news/news/article_4cec26a2-e0ec-11e3-813d-0019bb2963f4.html. Accessed 14 December 2019.

NC Policy Watch. 2016. Public can comment on Hofmann forest settlement. Available at: http://pulse.ncpolicywatch.org/2016/08/19/public-can-comment-on-hofmann-forest-settlement-between-epa-nc-state-resources-foundation/. Accessed 14 December 2019.

Olsen W. 2020. The Stupidest Einstein Meme. Commentary. Cato Institute. Available at: www.cato.org/publications/commentary/stupidest-einstein-meme. Accessed 22 February 2020.

Roosevelt TR. 1895. The higher life of American cities. A family paper. December 21, 1895. No. 1083. Available at: www.theodore-roosevelt.com/images/research/treditorials/o151.pdf Accessed 22 February 2020.

Sample SB. 2002. The Contrarian's Guide to Leadership. San Francisco (CA): Jossey-Bass. 197 p.

Watzin M. 2013. Hofmann Forest letter from Dean Mary Watzin. Available at: https://research.cnr.ncsu.edu/blogs/news/2013/01/23/hofmann-forest-letter-from-dean-mary-watzin/. Accessed 21 May 2021.

8 Conclusion

Purpose

The objective of this book was to present a brief and useful perspective on leadership and management for use by natural resource professionals and practitioners. The book has covered management, leadership, professionalism, and activism in natural resource management. I wrote from the perspective of a low- to middle-level line manager, as well as a senior elected officer in a professional organization, and an unusual role as an environmental activist, similar to a whistleblower.

In brief, the guiding principle for this book posits that leadership consists of aligning an organization's resources and actions with its stated intentions. This principle holds for natural resource leaders and managers, who have exceptional opportunities to enjoy fulfilling and rewarding work in either the public or private sector. We do, however, operate in complex systems of private and public lands, diverse goods and services, and social and governance demands that make identifying clear intentions and selecting approaches challenging. Leaders must assess their organizational context; develop and pursue a vision; muster resources and people; and employ genuine, fair, and transparent strategies and tactics to achieve organizational goals.

Sectoral Differences

Managers and leaders in the private sector seek to produce natural resource market goods and services at a profit and with a good return for landowners and investors who provide capital for their enterprises. They also jointly produce a wealth of nonmarket ecosystem services and can provide relatively unique valuable ESG benefits that may attract investors to their companies and to their land management opportunities. In addition private firms seek to receive government or private sector payments for the ecosystem

DOI: 10.4324/9781003141297-8

services they provide, whether through voluntary markets and negotiated exchanges or through mandatory regulatory markets (i.e., for carbon storage or biodiversity protection). Such payments, coupled with existing market returns, can make natural resources realize the full private and social values they provide to humans and ensure they are managed and protected wisely.

Leaders and managers in private markets must produce and manage their organizations and their market commodities efficiently and profitably, so that natural resources remain close to their optimal natural state and continue to help innovate in ways to capitalize on the potential of ecosystem services production and financial payments. These organizational methods must include a variety of land management approaches that retain and restore the native systems and natural ecosystems without adverse externalities or land degradation, not just maximizing commodity production at the least cost, but private firms also must receive adequate payment if wiser management methods occur or competition from exploitive producers or other land uses will cause land loss.

Leaders and managers in the public sector essentially start with a different mission of managing diverse natural resources and lands that have been politically reserved or purchased in order to protect their ecosystem values. They must manage these lands efficiently based on the policy directives and scarce budgets provided by their respective unit of government. Public sector management presumes that the ecosystems already are so valuable—or had so little value that they were not worth selling originally—that they should be owned and managed by the government at various levels from local to national. Public sector managers and leaders by definition then must be directly involved with and depend on political, social, and governance components of natural resource management. Their tasks focus on providing mostly nonmarket services and goods such as recreation; leisure; ecosystem services of water, air, and biodiversity, as well as some market goods such as timber, minerals, and developed recreation. Public land managers must be skilled in public processes and community management, and their agencies still rely on many organizational principles discussed in this book.

The host of nonprofit organizations, professional and trade associations, environmental/nongovernment organizations (E/NGOs), land conservancies, and related organizations also must meet the visions and missions of their sponsors, whether it be members, government funders, charitable gift organizations, or land users. They too must discern and respond to their funding sources and meet their program and financial obligations, largely through effective organizational management and leadership.

Leadership and management are means to constructively seek desirable missions, visions, and goals through well-organized processes and interaction among leaders, employees, staff, stakeholders, and customers. The management process is complex, as are the leaders, workers, and followers who participate in production of goods and services. Private firms in the natural resource sector must operate efficiently to make profits and reasonable returns on investment capital and meet rapidly evolving ESG goals; nonprofits may produce ecosystem services and some commodities, or advance professional, social, or environmental causes, but still have to break even and satisfy the same strictures. Public organizations must satisfy people, politicians, and land users and be efficient and decide how to spend scarce appropriations best. Great leadership and management are required for all of these missions.

Leadership Examples

I draw from Block (2017), Covey (1990), and others to define leadership as aligning resources and actions with stated intentions. The more that leaders can align their resources with the organizations' stated mission, the more success they will have, and vice versa. Leadership can occur at any level of an organization, at every stage of one's career, in a variety of line, volunteer NGO, and activist roles. Leadership starts with excellent performance in one's job due to talent, education, and dedication. It then translates into persons receiving more responsibilities and promotions to manage resources and people to achieve the mission of the organization at their respective level.

At their best, leadership and management offer large employment and personal opportunities for developing and applying one's professional interest and talents to make a positive difference and improve people's lives and social welfare. Leaders and managers can identify and do the right things. Advancing in one's career and having increasing opportunities to learn more, as well as determine and pursue meaningful and productive natural resource management outcomes, is a spiritually and intellectually rewarding path. And the farther one advances, the greater the opportunities there are to be a leader and to determine what actions can be taken and have greater impacts on improving the common good.

Leaders should have insights and communication with employees to perceive opportunities, problems, or issues with their organizations. In their jobs, leaders may have authority as a line manager (legitimate power), technical expert, or the respect and approval from followers (referent power), which they can use to develop best practices and actions. Professionals will find themselves in line, staff, and volunteer situations, with various missions, employees, natural resources, and budgets, and a mix of official and organizational powers and of different interest groups and stakeholders to satisfy.

At a global and national level, the chapter on natural resource leaders illustrates the success, rewards, and disappointments that every natural resource leader might have. Every professional person reviewed—from Ding Darling to Wangari Maathai to Bob Brown to Greta Thunberg—used their knowledge of natural resources and their voice to educate, inform, motivate, or lead immense positive changes in natural resource management and protection and more recently for women and diversity.

Each of these natural resource or environmental leaders perceived and tried to redress a variety of environmental problems ranging from overhunting and land destruction to large dams and climate change. And each have had conservation and career success, and some fame, but many struggles and disappointments and frustration. Moving from management to leadership to activism may have helped every person achieve broader impacts but also led to criticism and failure at times, as well as protecting natural resources and the environment became more challenging as the scale of development and human impacts on earth became greater.

So the leadership icons reviewed here bear a two-edged lesson for natural resource professionals—that one must balance vision, leadership, management, and activism with care both to be an effective and enduring leader where you are and when the time is right. Leadership for most professionals is more apt to be about doing your job well in your organization than changing the world. It always involves working with others to achieve your organizational missions and objectives, recognizing that many different opinions and courses of actions can be used to accomplish those missions, and serving your groups and teams in achieving that goal.

As low- to middle-level professionals and managers, you are not apt to start crusades often if ever and will be expected to implement organizational policy with some flexibility, but not autonomy. You will be a scientific and technical manager, well grounded in your discipline, augmented by social science and public process tools, organizational management principles, and personal experience.

My experience reflects that moderate opportunities for management and leadership change during one's career. I sought career advancement and served 13 years as line manager for research and education organizations. But middle management wears one out trying to satisfy challenging superiors and anxious employees with a small staff. Leadership as a nonprofit president followed my professional calling but was more contentious than anticipated. Leadership as an activist opposing an unwise university decision was an ethical but somewhat perilous choice. It did reflect similar choices that whistleblowers or others may reluctantly face in their employment or volunteer organizations.

Professional Implications

Professionals will have to be calm and deliberate managers and leaders to be effective in their organizations and careers. Differences of opinion about policies and practices will occur, complex personnel and budget issues will challenge one's skills, and conflicts over resource management and interest group opinions should be expected. It takes awareness and insight to recognize issues, courage to speak out and seek improvements to the status quo, skill to manage deliberations and resolve problems in your organizations and among your stakeholders, and wisdom to realize when to accept other opinions and approaches that are valid and useful.

In all of these types of shifting roles, a leader has to recognize issues, have and pursue a vision, muster resources and learn from and work with supportive colleagues, evaluate and reward success that meets the organizational mission and vision, and pursue every small detail to the best of one's ability. As a leader at NC State and SAF, I identified our service missions and visions collaboratively, established transparent benchmarks for evaluation, measured and evaluated progress, and rewarded individuals with the resources available. While perfection is not possible in all of these efforts, vision, talent, good faith, openness, and dedication can make a difference and can achieve reasonable goals for the management and protection of organizations, natural resources, and communities.

Virtually all successful leaders work very hard with good technical skills and with savvy networking and interpersonal skills. Leaders will advocate for and practice skillful work and equity. They must speak out calmly and lobby peers in and out of management meetings. They will have to be bold and persistent and resilient enough to withstand opposition and setbacks. Indeed, leaders will not always be pursuing the best or only "right" course and must listen, lose, and adapt to find successful natural resource management paths or indeed yield to the prevailing consensus of others with different opinions.

Successful leaders usually are fair and act with integrity. They respect individuals and diverse beliefs and rely on that diversity to generate broad and useful views and approaches and to connect with the diversity of natural resource users and interest groups. In natural resources, leaders will both manage the resources and protect them for future generations, per the principles of sustainable development.

Professionalism and leadership all are intermingled as one progresses in their career. Not all professionals actively seek advancement, upper management, and leadership, and in fact most prefer a reasonable and solid contribution in their jobs and professions. Even ambitious persons will eventually find that the ladder to the top is relatively short and limited and that professional growth in different positions at a given level, changes in employers, or even changes in careers are other paths to satisfaction. Everyone must balance their ambition, their ability to advance in their career, and their personal and professional interests.

Let me close with a few popular quotes about leadership that capture what it entails:

Eleanor Roosevelt (1960):

> You gain strength, courage, and confidence by every experience in which you really stop to look fear in the face. You are able to say to yourself, "I lived through this horror. I can take the next thing that comes along."

T.S. Eliot:

> "Trying is all that matters. Everything else is just not our business."
> (paraphrased by Gellman 2018)

Winston Churchill:

> Success is not final. Failure is not fatal. It is the courage to continue that counts.
> (Apocryphal; Quote Investigator 2013)

Leadership in natural resources includes all of these viewpoints and more. These popular quotes all are relevant to the points made here and are quoted as commonly stated. Only Eleanor Roosevelt's, however, seems to be stated in its original form. Eliot's is an abridged version of the dual merits of trying when writing and perhaps in life. Churchill's aphorism is sterling and was quoted at the end of a recent 2018 movie *The Darkest Days*. However, the quote investigator dissects it as it is being derived perhaps from Churchill, or perhaps an Anheuser Busch beer advertisement in the 1930s, or from two famous football coaches. Nonetheless, all three capture the challenge of leadership well—it is difficult; failure does occur; and persistence is mandatory to garner success, which is never permanent. Professional leadership and management certainly are challenges for a lifetime. Hopefully some of the principles and cases discussed in this book help illustrate useful approaches to achieve success.

References

Block P. 2017. *The Empowered Manager, Second Edition: Positive Political Skills at Work.* Hoboken (NJ): Wiley. 213 p.

Covey SR. 1990. *Principle-Centered Leadership.* New York: Free Press. 335 p.

Gellman M. 2018. Paraphrased quote from T.S. Eliot. God Squad: Rest assured you're not alone in trying to make a difference. New Haven Register. Available at: www.nhregister.com/religion/article/GOD-SQUAD-Rest-assured-you-re-not-alone-in-12753101.php. Accessed 18 February 2020.

Quote Investigator. 2013. Success is never final and failure never fatal. It's courage that counts. Quote incorrectly attributed to Winston Churchill. Available at: https://quoteinvestigator.com/2013/09/03/success-final/. Accessed 18 February 2020.

Roosevelt E. 1960. *You Learn by Living.* New York: Harper Perennial. 224 p.

Index

Printed in the United States
by Baker & Taylor Publisher Services